UPCOMING BOOKS IN 2015 AND 2016

by T.N. Carpenter

AS PART OF THE FINDING HAPPILY-EVER-AFTER SERIES:

Always a Bridesmaid, Now be a Bride

The Bride and Groom's Guide to What to Do Before, "I Do."

What's Your Happily-Ever-After?

For updates on these upcoming books, follow T.N. Carpenter at:

Facebook: www.facebook.com/pages/TN-Carpenter-Books
Twitter: Twitter.com/TN_Carpenter

Along The Way To Happily-Ever-After . . .

A Humorous Guide to Weathering the Newlywed Years and Creating a Happy and Lasting Marriage

T.N. CARPENTER

Along the Way to Happily-Ever-After. . . :
A Humorous Guide to Weathering the Newlywed Years and Creating a Happy and Lasting Marriage

The Finding Happily-Ever-After Series

Published by: The Writers' Café Publishing Group
www.writerscafepublishing.com

Cover and Interior Design by:
The Fast Fingers Book Formatting Service
www.thefastfingers.com

Contact T.N. Carpenter at:

Email: tn@tncarpenter.com
Website: www.alongthewaytohappilyeverafter.com
Facebook: www.facebook.com/pages/TN-Carpenter-Books
Twitter: Twitter.com/TN_Carpenter

dedication

To my husband, Jay. You are the love of my life and my "B.F.F." Thank you for encouraging me to "just write!" My dear husband, if it weren't for you, this book would not have been possible. I love you with all my heart.

acknowledgments

I would like to thank my mother-in-law and father-in-law, Marie and Joe, who just celebrated their 52nd wedding anniversary. Thank you for your contribution to this book.

Also, thank you to: G and P; Jennifer Anderson and Raymond Haight; Marianne and Paul; Janis Wilson Hughes and Rob Hughes; and Tomeka Jackson-Chance and Anson Chance. My dear friends, thank you for your contributions to this book by sharing your marital wisdom.

table of contents

table of contents

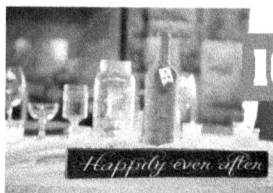

Happily-Ever-After?

"It is only possible to live happily ever after on a day-to-day basis."

-Margaret Bananno

prologue

After many years of hoping, dreaming, dating, and planning, you have found "The One," and it's your wedding day. You've said "I do," and you have committed yourself to spending the rest of your life with that special someone. You are married!

If you have a good wedding photographer, it is inevitable the photographer will capture a snapshot of you and your spouse with your backs to the camera. You are holding hands, both staring into the distance. This photograph symbolizes you and your loved one's first steps on your path toward the future you will now share as husband and wife. And what awaits as you embark upon your future together remains a mystery.

Take a moment and find that picture (and if you don't have that picture, find your favorite wedding picture of you and your spouse). Now, study that picture and think back. What were you thinking at that very moment as you began your future with your spouse? What was your idea of your future together? What was your idea of happily-ever-after? What was your spouse's idea?

As the years come and go, you will look back at that photograph and likely realize your path has not been that straight and perfect path into the sunset and the world of happily-ever-after you may have imagined. Especially during the newlywed years, there will be curves and bumps. Maybe even a dead-end to divorce for some. Perhaps, an intersection between insanity and delirium. Time will only tell. And maybe, that's what's so exciting (and scary) about marriage. When you mesh two people together, you never know what the other person is going to do, or what's around the bend.

It is almost inevitable that, along the way to "happily-ever-after," and especially during the newlywed years, there are going to be challenges. It takes strength, faith, commitment, and usually, a big sense of humor (and sometimes medication!) to face these obstacles head-on and remain committed to your marriage. The longer you're married, the more you will see that conquering the small, everyday challenges will help you create a strong marital foundation, and it makes it easier to triumph over the major hurdles and marital setbacks. And, along the way to "happily-ever-after," you may even learn a lesson or two, making you a better person and a better spouse, thereby creating a stronger marriage. And surprisingly, you will probably look back on many of your adventures and challenges, and actually be able to laugh about it.

As you read this book, you'll see I'm not perfect, and by no means is my marriage perfect, or will it ever be perfect. My husband and I have been together for nine years, and married for over seven years. Along the way to "happily-ever-after," we have seen the rich and the poor of "for richer or for poorer." We've thrived during the better, and endured the worst of "for better or for worse." I thought I caught a minor case of the "Seven-Year Itch." We've been battling infertility issues. Every day, we are still feeling our way through our marriage and learning by trial and error. And, I admit there are times when my own lessons learned and advice go right out the window, and I do something stupid.

So I, by no means, believe I should be on a pedestal, or that I know everything about marriage. But, I hope that by reading this book, you see that even if you and your spouse are not-so-perfect (like my husband and I), your marriage is far from perfect, and "happily-ever-after" isn't all you thought it was cracked up to be, you still can be happy and remain committed to making your marriage work.

This book encompasses the lessons I have learned as we have traveled along the way to "happily-ever-after." I hope after reading my adventures and lessons learned during the newlywed years, you too can remain committed to making your marriage last through any challenges you may experience in your marriage. Hopefully, you can laugh at and relate to my seemingly exaggerated tall tales and personal short stories about married life. And, perhaps, you can learn something from my tidbits and advice. Agree or agree to disagree with me. However, I hope you smile, laugh, and maybe even learn something that will help you on your path to your happily-ever-after!

Chapter One

25 Basic Ingredients:
A Starter Recipe for a Happy and Lasting Marriage

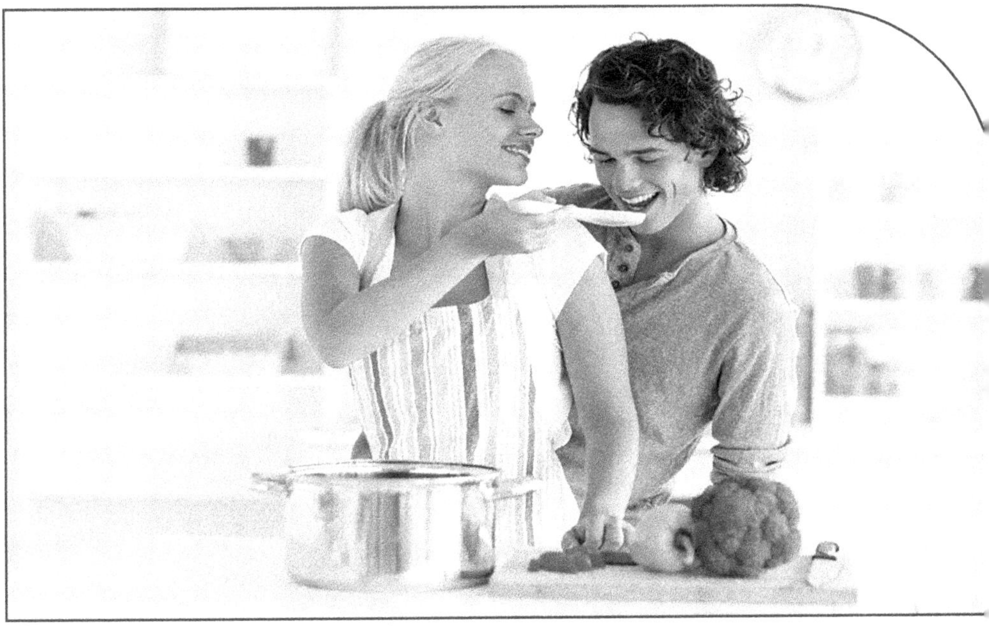

You probably believe this lovely little book on marriage will begin with that special moment after you have taken your vows—right when you are pronounced husband and wife, your wedding guests cheer and clap, the doves are released, and rose petals and bubbles fill the air. Well, not just yet! The steps to happily-ever-after begin long before you say, "I do." There are certain personality and relationship traits you will need to help ensure compatibility and ensure you and your loved one are heading in the same direction along your path to happily-ever-after.

Like a great recipe, there are some ingredients you and your significant other need to make sure you have stashed away to ensure your marriage does not end up falling flat, creating a recipe for disaster. Like a good recipe, depending upon conditions and your individual tastes, the measurements and directions will have to be tweaked here and there. Maybe a little more of one thing and a little less of another. Sometimes you and your partner will have to "eye" your mixture and add or subtract ingredients to make sure it's the right consistency. However, as long as you have these basic ingredients, you will be on the right track.

Basic Ingredients

A heart full of *Love*
A bowl full of *Commitment*
Two cups of *Loyalty*
Three cups of *Unconditional Love*
Two cups of *Chemistry*
Four cups of *Friendship*
One cup of *Acceptance*
Two large bowls of *Respect*
A hand full of *Understanding*
Plenty of *Romance*
A baker's dozen of *Honesty*
A lot of *Heart and Soul*
A pinch of *Independence*
A tablespoon full of *Spunk*
A dose of *Patience*
A little *Creativity*
A splash of *Humor*
A dash of *Selflessness*
One can each of *Empathy and Sympathy*
A bottle of *Open-Mindedness*
A package of *Optimism*
A bucket of *Communication*
One bag of *Trust*
A batch of *Faith*
A sprinkle of *Shared Dreams*

Directions:

1. Make sure you and your loved one have all these ingredients because just having ***love*** for one another will not be enough. As you begin to mix your recipe for a lasting and happy marriage, remember that a memorable dish is not great just because of the ingredients, but also because it is made with ***heart and soul***.
2. So, before "I do," begin mixing these ingredients and let them simmer. As it simmers, you and your loved one may need to conduct several taste tests with your recipe so that you can figure out if you need a little more of one ingredient, and a little less of another. It may take adjusting this recipe a few times, but as time passes, you will know just the right combination so that your marriage turns out "just right." However, here are the basics.
3. Trust me, when you take your vows, nerves and emotions will kick in. It will happen so quickly, you hardly will remember what you said until later when you are watching yourself on your wedding video. Realize, that the "for better or for worse, for richer or for poorer, and in sickness and in health" are not just words. It means something. You have to look at your spouse and know 100%, and believe in your heart 100%, without a doubt, that you are ***committed*** to this person. Not only should you remain committed during the "better," but should there come a time when you two are enduring the "worse," you must be determined to still stay committed and make your marriage work. In order to do this, you have to come to some realizations and make some acknowledgments.
4. You must recognize that no one is perfect. Neither you, nor your loved one will ever be perfect. We are human, and you each have to be prepared that there will be some times, actually *lots* of times, when your spouse (and you) will make mistakes, or do something really stupid. But, that's why you must have the ingredients of ***unconditional love*** and ***acceptance***. Through ***unconditional love*** comes ***acceptance*** because no matter what, good or bad, you love that person. With these ingredients, even when you see the bad in your spouse, or the mistakes he or she has made, you will remain ***loyal*** to your spouse and ***committed*** to remain together.
5. These ingredients don't help for just the big "oops" that can happen. These ingredients get you through the everyday imperfections of

morning breath, bad gas, bad hair, and PMS. It helps one to overlook the other being messy, one being a horrible cook, or when you say regretful things. You love each other when one is beautiful, when one looks a hot mess, or when one has gained 25 pounds.

6. ***Unconditional love*** comes from not just having a lot of ***chemistry*** and ***romance*** between one another, but more importantly by having a ***friendship*** and a bond that no man can put asunder. Realize that this friend will be there 24/7 for the rest of your life. So make sure your spouse is not just your best friend, but your "B.F.F."
7. Regardless, you must have ***respect*** for your partner. You don't degrade or demean them. You have an ***open mind*** and an ***open heart***, and you ***respect*** your differences. By respecting your differences, you won't try to change each other. Also, you will ***understand*** why your spouse is different, and understand their weaknesses, fears, hopes, and goals. You will be there to support one another. To be able to do this, you must be ***selfless*** and realize your marriage is not just about you. If you don't have ***empathy***, then you must have ***sympathy***.
8. In order to have ***understanding***, you must be able to ***communicate*** with one another. This is not just talking and hearing, this is *speaking* and *listening*. This is not implicitly communicating, but *explicitly* communicating.
9. Realize that no one is a mind reader, and out of all your differences, it is important to remember that men and women think differently. Because we think, perceive, and process things differently, it is important to be clear and explicit in order to communicate. But, you have to learn to *effectively* communicate with one another. This usually isn't through yelling and screaming. There are effective methods of communication to help you each respond more positively. Figure it out and try to communicate in that manner.
10. Effective ***communication*** in combination with ***unconditional love, acceptance,*** and ***respect*** opens the door to ***honesty***. The more ***honesty*** there is, the easier it is to ***trust*** one another. When you ***trust*** each other like no other person, you have an undying ***loyalty*** and a strong ***commitment*** to each other.
11. ***Accept*** that there will be difficult times in your marriage. It will not be

all sunshine, hugs, and kisses. This is when the ingredient of ***patience*** will be important. If you ***trust*** that your spouse is ***committed*** to you and your marriage, it is easier to be ***patient*** and be all the more ***determined*** to get through your tough time together. If you ***love*** each other, and you each are ***determined*** to stay ***committed,*** have ***faith*** that you will get through the hard times, move past the "worse," and return to the "better."

12. In an effort to see more "better" than "worse," your marriage must be filled with the ***optimism*** that when working together, you both can achieve and accomplish anything. But be secure with each other having their own ***independence*** and a ***little spunk*** so you each don't lose your individual identities. That way, you won't constantly have the expectation that your spouse must complete you in every way or fulfill your every need because, realize, you will *never* have that with *anyone*.
13. Also, be ***creative*** and have ***shared dreams*** to aim for. These two ingredients will keep you going when you hit those inevitable patches of boredom and monotony. The ingredients of ***commitment*** and ***unconditional love*** will be important during these times too.
14. Last, but not least, while you are creating your dish for a happy and lasting marriage, here are a few optional ingredients that I recommend: ***don't sweat the small stuff*** and ***have a sense of humor***! Sometimes, when you are going through the worst, the poorer, the sickness, and the unexpected, all you may have is laughter and your ***unconditional love*** and ***commitment*** to one another.
15. Happy mixing!

advice

The Five-Ingredient Relationship Rescue Recipe:

Sometimes, we need specific ingredients from our spouse to uplift us or give us support. However, most of the time, our loved ones won't know exactly what we need unless we expressly tell them. Therefore, when you have those moments, below is a cute little way to expressly tell your spouse what you need. It can be used in the evenings after a long day, during a rough patch, or after experiencing a personal or marital setback.

My loved one, right now, I need from you (ingredients):

____

____

____

____

____

Because: ____

____

____

____

Chapter Two

The Honeymoon is Over, Now What?

Suggested Ingredients: Patience; Commitment; Humor; Acceptance; Loyalty; Understanding; Communication; Faith; and Optimism.

Tall Tales

Now that the honeymoon is over, it's time for you and your loved one to enjoy wedded bliss wherever you call home. Home could be your loved one's place, your place, or a new place. Wherever it is, once you live together, it is time to merge the tastes and styles of a woman and a man (oh, dear!).

For women, it is likely you probably know the difference between travertine and ceramic tile, quartz and granite counters, or oak and maple cabinets. You know the difference between sea mist green and sea foam green or oil-rubbed bronze fixtures and brushed-nickel fixtures. You know about crown molding, wainscotting, and accent colors. You understand the concepts of Feng Shui and symmetry.

However, for men, they know only the five primary colors. A man's idea of furnishings always involves black leather furniture; and the bigger, older, and more comfortable the furniture is, the better. Men do not care anything about granite or types of tiles or cabinets. Whatever is the absolute cheapest is the best choice. However, most men know everything about electronics. No penny is ever spared for the top-of-the line flat screen, surround sound, computer system, or smartphone.

Ladies, when you move in together, your loved one will show up with very few things. He will not even require a moving truck. He will have packed two black trash bags and three boxes in his car. One black trash bag will hold all his clothes. The other black trash bag will hold all the left-over personal hygiene items, magazines, and anything else he could not put in the three boxes that he actually packed (I have never understood this universal idea that men have to just pack away stuff in black garbage bags).

He will have two boxes that hold his video game consoles, blue ray players, surround sound system, CDs, DVDs, video games, sports memorabilia, and a couple trophies from high school. His third box will contain all his kitchen items including: three mis-matched dinner plates; two plastic cups; a beer mug, and one mixing bowl that was used not only for mixing, but also to eat cereal; Ramen noodles; and soup. His kitchen utensils and cookware will be comprised of one spatula, a wooden spoon, one frying pan with a broken handle, one large pot, a rusted cookie sheet, and a mis-matched silverware serving set for one.

His four largest items will be transported by one of his friends who has a truck. These items will be: a couch or futon that a charitable organization wouldn't accept as a donation; a piece of gym equipment he probably hasn't used at least since he met you; his flat-screen TV; and a mattress and box spring (with no bed frame).

Women, on the other hand, we require a large moving truck. Ladies, you know you will have at least one-hundred labeled and neatly packed boxes. All fragile items will be wrapped in bubble wrap and packed in boxes filled with Styrofoam peanuts. Due to years of anticipation of the day you would move in with your loved one, you will have stockpiled everything that you could ever need for a home and then some.

You have packed away your everyday china and your special occasion china. You have small appliances like an espresso machine (although you never drink espresso), a rice cooker, and a food processor. You will possess every kitchen gadget right down to the lemon peel grater and the melon ball scooper. You have a full set of hard-anodized cookware, including a grill pan, a paella pan, and a wok. You have sheets, duvets, and matching curtains. Of course, you bring a decorated shower curtain to match your bath rugs and toothbrush holder. You have throw pillows, rugs, quilts, candles, paintings, lamps, vases, baskets, and decorated picture frames. However, at least one half of the truck will hold your clothes, shoes, and purses.

Your husband thought that moving in together would take about three hours, but once he sees the size of the moving truck you rented and the number of boxes you have packed, he immediately realizes this will be a three-*day* process (and he's going to have to bribe some buddies with beer to come help out). Of course, you will expect that by the end of the weekend, all items are unpacked and all the furniture is in its correct place of which you have spent hours diagraming while anticipating your moving in together.

Ladies, at this point, you will have so overwhelmed your new hubby with your boxes and furniture that his two trash bags and three boxes cannot compete. This will be the moment your husband realizes that he will never again have a place decorated in a manner he likes (well, this is probably a good thing!).

In addition to the drastic adjustments that come along with moving in together, there will be adjustments to actually living together under the same roof and adjusting to each other's good and bad sides, quirks, and idiosyncrasies. Before you move in together, life with your partner is like an eternal date. You cannot wait to spend time with one another. When you are dating, if you're in a bad mood, you can fake a good mood because it is easy to be on your best behavior for a few hours. Plus, you're happy to see your loved one. If you're messy, you can clean up your place because your loved one is your guest.

For women, when we are dating, we will always fix ourselves up, wear make-up, and look our best. Men will be cleanly-shaven, wear their best button-down shirt and pants, and carry the scent of designer cologne. Men will sit through chick flicks, and women will cuddle with their man while he watches a sporting event. You will cook together, and you two will have long conversations that begin with dinner and wine and will last until the early hours of morning.

All this time, while you are "wooing" one another, you do not realize the other person's faults and the things that one day you will have to learn to live with . . . live with, 24/7, *til death do you part*. Once you begin living together, things will change quite drastically. For every one cute thing you love about your partner, there now will be about five things you did not realize about them before living together that you will despise.

Ladies, as for your husband, you will learn that he cleaned up real nice for your dates, but now that you are married, you will realize that his regular wardrobe includes about 50 different T-shirts, a couple pairs of basketball shorts, a pair of tennis shoes, two pairs of jeans, one dress shirt, and one pair of khakis. So most days, his preferred attire will include a T-shirt with some ridiculous phrase splattered on it and a pair of shorts. He does not know how to put the lid down on the toilet. He has piles of sports magazines, electronics, and sports equipment. If he knew how to cook before he met you, he will suffer from amnesia and not know how to make anything other than a bowl of cereal.

He will watch the sports channel for hours on end. He won't have time to take out the garbage, but he will spend hours washing and waxing his car. He will insist he does not need to read the instructions for anything that needs assembling. Therefore, it will take him four times longer to assemble something than it would have taken if he would have just read the instructions (and, there will be extra screws and parts leftover).

While he managed to have decent table manners when you were dating, such as eating with a fork and knife, slowly sipping a drink, and quietly chewing his food, he will now eat a full plate of food in about 90 seconds flat (usually without silverware) and chew food with his mouth open. You will now hear scary sounds come from his mouth and butt that are followed by deathly odors. And, even scarier, if you see him carrying a newspaper or magazine into the bathroom, you know the toxic odors that will seep from under the door may require evacuation (and you may need to call your local HAZMAT team).

But, ladies, men are not the only ones with hidden issues. Husbands have to learn to live with 1/10 of a closet because we must have the remaining 9/10 of the closet, plus another closet to store all of our clothes, shoes, and purses. While his side of the bathroom counter contains a toothbrush, razor, and a bottle of shaving cream, our side will be inundated with soaps, lotions, astringent, moisturizers, make-up, a blow dryer, flat iron, curling iron, hair spray, mousse, and gel. Our tampons and maxi pads will take up his bathroom cabinet space along with our footbath and pedicure kit. We will have a variety of shampoos, conditioners, face masks, and body scrubs draping the shower or bathtub. Of course, our hair will be everywhere. While we women never would have allowed our husbands to see us without makeup before marriage, our husbands will not only see us without makeup, but see us prancing around with a clay mask or cream hair remover on our faces.

Your husband will realize he can do no right, and he will get blamed for everything. He will learn that you spend your free time alternating between talking for hours on end on the telephone with your best friend or your mother. And, your husband will become increasingly concerned that on Sundays, you sit for hours watching lovely shows about weddings, house hunting, and having babies, but conclude the evening with several episodes of *Snapped* and *Wives with Knives*.

While they may not have been apparent before you began living together, your differences will almost instantaneously become apparent when you are living with each other seven days a week. One of you may be a morning person, while the other is not. One is always five minutes early, and the other is always at least a half an hour late. One is a couch potato, and the other is a gym rat. One is cold, the other hot. It takes 15 minutes for him to shower and get ready, and it takes you at least 1 hour and 15 minutes to get ready if you don't wash your hair.

One eats in bed, while the other does not. One snacks in between meals, while the other eats only at specially-designated times. One likes to stay up late and watch TV, while the other wants lights out and no sounds after 10:00 p.m. One snores loudly while the other stays awake contemplating smothering the other with a pillow. One is a neat freak; the other is a pack rat.

Additionally, things change. Once, your weekends were consumed with weekend trips, dinner dates, or enjoying happy hour or a movie. But the "wooing" stage is definitely over. **As married life sets in, there are chores to divide and complete around the house, necessary trips to the home-improvement store, grocery shopping to do, and bills to pay.**

You will no longer have those long, romantic conversations over dinner. Instead, you two will argue over whether you are going to watch the sports channel or a home decorating show during dinner. And ladies, regardless of what you two agree to watch, you make sure to turn up the volume to drown out your husband's lip smacking while he eats, and you will talk yourself out of stabbing him in the neck with your fork.

And, fellows, you will miss the idea of dead silence because, now, as soon as you arrive home, your wife will bombard you with stories. While you listened to every word she had to say before you lived together, her long-winded stories that she tells every day will drive you insane. You will develop a glazed-over look, pretend to listen, but actually zone her out as you beg her in your head to please wrap up this story so you can catch the sports highlights.

So, men are from Mars, and women are from Venus, and how on earth do the two worlds mesh together? Take a deep breath. Don't throw your hands up and start packing up your loved one's stuff and kick them out. Rest assured that your two worlds can become one if you follow these five steps.

advice

Five Steps to Living in Harmony:

1. Step One: Do not let your petty differences cause you to lose focus of the big picture. Just because you and your spouse were destined to be together does not mean you are exactly the same. We are all individuals, and we have our differences, bad habits, and pet peeves.

The little pet peeves you have about each other will be the elephant in the room in the beginning. They will be most apparent because these little idiosyncrasies are new to you, and they are driving you ABSOLUTELY INSANE! But, focus, and literally, don't sweat the small stuff! Keep telling yourself that these are *petty* differences. Look around at everything else you have in common, and that will outweigh the small differences.

Realize that no matter whom you live with, there are going to be things about them that will make your blood boil. No matter who it is, no two people are exactly alike. When sharing space with anyone, we all have to compromise, adapt, and accept things we don't like. So, better your partner than someone else!

2. Step Two: Compromise, Compromise, COMPROMISE. I am being realistic when I tell you it is unlikely that you and your loved one are going to change all your old ways and habits just to please the other. It is not necessarily because we are stubborn; it is just that we all have our bad habits. And truthfully, at a certain age, even if we want to change, most of us are too set in our ways. But, before you go into a rage because your loved one has failed to change some certain annoying habit, realize your spouse does not want to be changed any more than you want them changing you.

Likely, you will have to resort to compromise. And by compromise, I mean learning to accept your partner's quirks in exchange for them accepting your quirks. Realize that however frustrating it may be for you to get used to living with your partner, it will be equally frustrating for them to adjust living with you. For instance, men detest their wives' makeup, shampoo bottles, and body washes lying all over the place as much as women cannot stand their husbands' sports magazines, T-shirts, and tools laying around. You both will have to "test the waters" and determine what each of you can tolerate and what will push you past your boiling points.

3. Step Three: Testing the waters: trial and error. Most things will appear to be petty differences, and through compromise, you will learn to live with the idiosyncrasies of your partner, and vice versa. However, no matter how petty some things will seem, there will be boundary lines drawn and unspoken ground rules laid about some behaviors that cannot be overlooked by the other no matter how petty it may seem to one who is guilty of the behavior. For instance, my husband and I prefer different coffee creamers, so we each buy our own. Yet, when my husband would use all his creamer, he would then proceed to use all my creamer, but not replace it. So, one Saturday morning after I almost self-combusted over my practically empty coffee creamer carton that he used, but had not replaced, my husband quickly realized that although using all my coffee creamer seemed minor to him, it was a boundary he should not cross if he didn't want me to reach a boiling point. It can be something like knowing your loved one needs space in the evenings after work to just unwind, or that you can't stand a cup to be used without a coaster. The waters are tested, and once we realize how important something is to the other, no matter how trivial it may seem, we usually can adjust accordingly.

4. Step Four: Be patient and allow for a period of adjustment. I will be the first to admit that attempting to compromise is much easier said than done! It is not easy, and for the things about your spouse that still make you want to scream, take a deep breath, give it time, and allow for a period of adjustment. It may take time for you and your loved one to get used to living with one another. If the first few weeks or months are difficult, don't give up.

Did you ever have to share a room with a messy, stinky sibling who snored? Or, did you ever share a dorm room or apartment with a weird, obnoxious roommate? If you survived that, then surely, you and your loved one can get past your differences and learn to live together.

As time passes, you will adjust, learn to accept your differences, and adapt to this new dynamic. As you adjust, the petty differences will really begin to seem petty, and the things you love about your partner will overshadow the things you dislike. Living together will become easier. Without even knowing it, the unspoken rules of your relationship will be created!

5. Step Five: Recognize and appreciate the creation of unspoken rules. Finally, if you are patient, you each compromise, and allow for a period of adjustment, with little or no effort, the automatic creation of unspoken rules will begin to occur. Without knowing it, or even saying anything to one another, magically, you each will adjust to each other's habits, faults, and imperfections. Also, the ground rules will be laid where you each have tested the waters and boundaries of one another, and you know each other's limits. For example, your significant other may know not to talk to you in the morning until you have had your coffee, or you know that your loved one hates it when the temperature gets above 74 degrees in your home.

Someway, somehow, it just happens. The more you and your spouse adapt and accept each other's differences, the more you will love each other because that person knows and understands you, good and the bad, more than anyone else. And, you will realize just how compatible you are because you love each other **despite** all the differences you have. So, just be patient, and let love and life take care of the petty differences.

short stories

Before my husband and I moved in together, he had lived by himself for over ten years, and it was difficult for him to get accustomed to sharing physical space with someone, especially a woman, who adds a whole different dynamic.

So after the trauma of actually moving our stuff into our first place together, my husband had an eye-opening experience about how challenging it is even when you are living with the person you love. He realized I was not a morning person, and after a few mornings of being cooly shot down after attempting to strike up conversation, he stopped and simply would kiss me on the cheek and say "good-bye" when he left for work. In the evening, after work, he, who is a neat freak, realized that I am not quite so neat.

He would come home from work and look in horror at my unopened mail piling up at the entryway desk. He would trip over my high-heeled shoes I had kicked off in the middle of the living room floor after coming home from work. He would go to our bedroom to neatly put away all his stuff, while my laundry laid unfolded in a laundry basket. He would walk to the bathroom to wash his hands, and my make-up took up all the counter space. Plus, my husband, who at the time, was not a cat person, also had to adjust to not just living with me, but also, my cat.

After about three weeks of living together, my husband finally broke down and vented about how he did not know that living together would be so hard. In frustration, he exclaimed he could not understand why I had so much stuff everywhere. Why couldn't I just pick up my stuff?

In response, I pointed out that living with him was not the easiest either. It drove me insane that every evening while I was cooking, he was glued to the TV watching sports highlights. I despised how he made a lumpy bed. Plus, my husband, who is a drummer, was always tapping to the beats in his head. Seriously, tapping at the dinner table, tapping at the computer desk, tapping on the steering wheel as he drove; the man does not know how to sit still, and it just makes me nervous! And, I couldn't stand the fact our place was lit up like a Christmas tree because he would leave a room without turning off the lights.

At that moment, my husband realized living together was just as much of an adjustment for me as it was for him. He realized we both had imperfections, faults, and pet peeves. So, after we each recognized we both had dislikes about the other's habits, the compromising began.

For instance, in exchange for my husband accepting my piles of unfolded laundry, I tried not to make a big deal about his inability to make the bed. And other things, we changed. My husband's neatness began to rub off on me. I would see his neat side of the bathroom counter, and the sight of my messy side of the counter made me want to clean up my clutter. Through testing the waters, we knew each other's limits and boundaries, like that I need silence in the morning (and creamer for my coffee!), and my husband needs to unwind in the evening by watching sports highlights.

And, yet other things, we adapted. There came a point that we just accepted each other's differences, and we learned to live together. Either it is acceptance (or delusional denial), but now, he is oblivious to my piles of unopened mail, and I automatically turn off the lights he has left on throughout the house.

More importantly, we began to appreciate just how much we began to know about one another, and there came the creation of unspoken rules. It just happened. I can't tell you how, or why, but we just adapted. Some way, somehow, years have passed, and my shoes are still laid out in the middle of the living room floor and there are still baskets of unfolded laundry. My husband still makes the worst, lumpiest bed I've ever seen. But, for the most part, we don't even pay attention or even see the differences anymore. All these years later, after we first moved in together, instead of letting the petty differences be the elephant in the room and thinking about how different we are, we recognize and appreciate how, even with our differences, we complement and accept one another.

We constantly think of the same thing at the same time. We can finish each other's sentences. We have inside jokes that no one else would understand, nor would we dare ever tell anyone. When we travel, no matter where we stay, it is completely unconscious, but I will automatically take the right side of the bed, and he takes the left. We rarely say what we are wearing out somewhere, and somehow, we will get ready at the same exact time and coordinate perfectly.

Petty differences, major pet peeves, and all, there is nowhere else I'd rather be, and no one else I'd rather be with. Without a doubt, I know this man knows and appreciates me, good and bad. And good and bad, this is *our* life and *our* home. Exactly where I belong. Knowing exactly where we belong is worth the lumpy beds, the unfolded laundry, the messy bathroom counters, the imaginary drum tapping, endless sports events, and the moody mornings.

As time passes, if it grows easier to live together, you are getting through your period of adjustment. Be patient. Once your unspoken rules begin to develop, it will feel wonderful to have someone who loves you and knows you more than anyone else, good and bad. If you love one another, you will find a way to learn to live together.

advice

Quick, Five-Minute Exercises for Blissful Wedded Benefits:

Until you get to the point where you either hit delusional denial, or you are in eternal marital bliss, here is a five-minute exercise that will eliminate marital tension and maximize marital strength. You won't even have to get off the couch or pull out the weights because this is all mental. This gives a new meaning to "mind over matter" because it's just a matter of not focusing on all the little negative things about your spouse that probably don't really matter in the whole scheme of your marriage.

1. Let go: Most of us want to always have complete control over a situation or our lives. We must realize we cannot have control over everything, including our significant others. In fact, most of the time, we have no control over most outside influences, factors, and people, which includes our loved ones. The quicker you realize you cannot control everything, and you are wasting energy trying to control what cannot be controlled, the more time you will have to enjoy life for what it is. And, the more time you will have to focus on the positive aspects of your marriage and what you love about your spouse.

2. Acceptance: Remember, acceptance is one of the basic ingredients you need in your relationship. If you try to control someone, sooner or later, they are going to resent you for trying to change them and for not accepting them for who they are. So, here is a way to recognize the ways your partner has accepted you; and hence, why you should accept your partner:

I must realize that although it may be easy for me to judge my loved one for their bad habits, I must recognize that my loved one has learned to accept my own bad habits, which include:

____

____

____

____

____

And for all the bad habits we both have, the following good traits about my partner outweigh their bad habits:

____

____

____

____

Chapter Three

50/50: The Collective Bargaining Process for Household Chores

Suggested Ingredients: Respect; Selflessness; Patience; Humor; and Communication.

Tall Tales

Before you lived together, you probably willingly helped each other out with household chores. You two probably went grocery shopping together to pick up ingredients for meals and then cooked together while you sipped wine.

So, once you began living together and settled into married life, it would seem that you two would help each other out more and more, and life would become so much easier because you are splitting chores 50/50. Right? Not likely! Here are my thoughts on keeping the responsibility from falling on just one person—you.

short stories

For the most part, I have always been lucky in that my husband is willing to help out with house cleaning. Every Sunday, we have our normal routine of cleaning the house, and usually, we can manage to clean the house with little or no arguments over who is going to clean what. However, recently, a moment of that just *expecting* me to cook and clean slipped out of my husband's mouth.

Not too long ago, I was working extremely long days and nights, and needless to say, our place was a mess. However, ironically, as I was spending late hours at work, my husband was sitting at home, watching the basketball play-offs. I was too tired to even complain. I could care less what the house looked like or what he was doing.

One Thursday evening, it was 8:00 at night, and I was heading back to my office to meet a deadline for the next day, and I knew it was going to be a long night.

As I walked out the door to endure this inevitably long night, my husband stood there (with the basketball game playing on the TV in the background) and told me, "*We* are going to have to clean this weekend. This place is a *pig sty*." What?!! @#!&*?!!!!! Well, I won't be able to tell you the foul words that came out of my mouth in response to this statement he had the nerve to make to me, but it ended with "*I* am not cleaning this weekend. *You* can clean!"

It could've been worse. He could've implied that just *I* should clean that weekend. However, how could he be so oblivious to what I had been doing (working endless hours) as opposed to him sitting around watching basketball every evening? I was fuming over his complete insensitivity, his inability to comprehend how tired I might be, and that maybe he should conclude that since he had time to watch basketball games in the evening, he could chip in and clean the house himself. So, that weekend, I was on strike. I was not cleaning anything just to prove my point, and after the foul-mouth words that came out of my mouth earlier, my husband knew not to mention that I clean again. Ultimately, my husband saw things in a different light and realized how insensitive this statement was. We worked things out, and the house cleaning duties resumed (at a later date *after* that weekend).

But, there are so many more women out there who don't experience this insensitivity once in a while, but *every* day. As you read this, you may have a similar experience. You are under-appreciated for the super spouse you are. You work, you clean, you cook, and you take care of the kids. Whatever your spouse is contributing, it is far from it being 50/50. And to be fair, as women, we usually want perfection when it comes to housecleaning. So, when our husbands do attempt to help us, instead of showing gratitude, we become critical that they didn't fold the towels the way we like them, or they didn't make the bed with hospital corners. This, in return, is a recipe for a husband who throws his hands up and questions why he should even bother helping if what he helps out with is never good enough. Either way, one or both of you are going to start resenting the other.

At some point, the resentment for being undervalued, unappreciated, and taken for granted has to reach a boiling point. After my strike, I realized that assigning household chores is really a bargaining process. So, here is a way to try to make the household responsibilities approximately 50/50.

advice

1. A common case of amnesia. Although you and your loved one gladly helped one another out while you were wooing and impressing one another, sometimes, once you are married, at least one partner will suffer from amnesia (uh hum... usually, the husband). They forget how to cook. They forget they need to take out the garbage on Thursday nights. They forget that someone has to buy groceries, and someone has to clean. They forget that floors need to be waxed, shelves dusted, dishes washed, clothes folded, and counters scrubbed. Basically, they forget, in general, that things around the house do not get done unless someone takes care of it. Maybe they don't forget, but instead, they assume the other will take over *all* the household responsibilities: cooking, dishes, cleaning, laundry, folding, and, grocery shopping.

However, to be fair, ladies, we forget things too. We forget how to assemble even the simplest item. We forget how to take out the garbage, and we don't know anything about checking oil, mowing a lawn, cleaning a pool (or any outdoor work for that matter), or lifting anything that weighs more than 10 pounds.

Hopefully, between all the things that you and your spouse will each forget, it will be about 50/50 as to the things you each will still remember to do. However, if you are handling it all, here's a collective bargaining process to help you get at least close to 50/50.

2. Strike! Several times a year, there are news stories where workers don't believe they are being fairly rewarded for the work they do. So, they protest. If this falls upon deaf ears, they strike. When the job is not getting done because the workers have stopped working, the employer's deaf ears miraculously open up, and they begin to listen. The lines of communication open and talks commence. And then begins the collective bargaining process where the parties begin negotiating. Giving a little to get a little so everyone can once again be happy and operations will resume.

To prevent a strike, as soon as you and your loved one begin living together, sit down and begin a collective bargaining process to ensure you both are doing your fair share around your place, and neither one believes they are being undervalued or under appreciated.

3. Collective Bargaining: I'll agree to this, if you agree to that. During collective bargaining, the negotiations will begin, and it will be time to pick and choose which responsibilities that each spouse will handle. This is not a cut-and-dry, simple process. You are merely trying to come to an agreement as to which chores you are willing to handle in exchange for your partner handling other responsibilities.

To ensure that negotiations continue and you don't reach an impasse, begin with making a list where you each split the chores by you taking the responsibilities you don't mind handling or can live with, and your spouse volunteering for those responsibilities he does not mind handling. Hopefully, your spouse won't mind handling some chores you don't like and vice versa. For instance, I love cooking and prefer to cook, but I hate cleaning up afterwards. My husband prefers that I cook (Well, I must admit, I am a better cook!), but he doesn't mind loading the dishwasher, so he will clean up after dinner. We are able to take on some chores we don't mind in exchange for ones we don't like, and both sides can be happy, and the whole task of cooking dinner and cleaning up afterwards can be completed.

By beginning with picking and choosing the easy stuff first, the chores you each don't mind doing, it shows an effort to reach a resolution. No arguments will begin over the chores you each volunteer to do, and thus, negotiations will continue instead of an immediate walk-out occurring.

Most importantly, if you are someone who is picky about how something should be cleaned or cooked, then it is probably best you agree to take that chore. For instance, as you are aware, I hate a lumpy bed. While I am good at making the bed up perfectly with hospital corners and every pillow in just the right place, I am terrible at making coffee. So, to make things easier, my husband makes the coffee in the morning, and I make up the bed. Problem solved.

However, after the easy part is over, it's time for concessions.

4. Concessions. In this process, no one is getting what they truly want. It will be a matter of coming to an agreement you both can live with so that normal household operations continue. There will be some responsibilities that you both hate, or rather, detest, *i.e.*, for my husband and me, scrubbing the soap scum off the ceramic tiles in the shower, cleaning the litter box, and shampooing the carpet. For those household chores you both despise, it's a draw. Whether it is drawing out of a hat, or a game of Rock, Paper, Scissors, you just have to assign those mutually detested tasks so that hopefully, it turns out about 50/50.

For my husband and me, we alternate handling those hated responsibilities each week. Usually, one will agree to take on a couple extra items on the cleaning list in exchange for the other handling the mutually-hated chore. As you know by now, you have to give some to get some.

5. Impasse. At some points, you may reach an impasse on some items. However, just because you reach an *impasse* doesn't mean all agreed-upon negotiations are off the table. As long as normal household daily operations continue to some extent, you can work on whatever you've accomplished. You can continue negotiations at any time on those *impasse* items. Or, like negotiations in the real world, if one person holds out long enough, the other will just give in.

For instance, as you know by now, I *despise* folding laundry. My husband doesn't like folding laundry either. So, usually, we hit an *impasse* on that chore. Therefore, unfolded laundry will sit in a basket for days, maybe even weeks. However, we continue completing other tasks, and finally, at some point, one of us gets fed up with the unfolded, clean laundry and will break down and fold it. Sometimes it's me, sometimes it's him.

6. Re-Negotiations. This collective bargaining process may not necessarily be a formal sit-down process of list making. The negotiation process may just begin to occur on a cleaning day as you begin to divide the cleaning list. It won't be set in stone, and it may change from week-to-week depending upon the circumstances. So, make sure you always leave room for re-negotiations at a later time.

7. Appreciating each other's contributions. Similar to the labor world, discussions cease and strikes occur because one or both sides believes they are being undervalued. This can also occur with household responsibilities, resulting in a shutdown (or a meltdown). Sometimes, just a willingness to help out and the ability to appreciate what the other is contributing makes all the difference. For instance, my husband folds towels in a way I don't like. When we were first married, I would let out a loud groan and go back and refold the towels. However, I began to realize how insensitive that was, and I have learned to bite my tongue, keep them the way he folded them (especially since I hate folding anyway!), and just be appreciative he volunteered to fold them. And, that opened up the door to him helping me with other things around the house because I'm not being critical about his household cleaning skills.

Realize that it probably never will be 50/50. No one is going to get exactly what they believe they deserve, and there will be times when you feel or will have to do more than your fair share. But the value of teamwork is priceless and showing appreciation toward one another's efforts goes a long way.

The "Honey Do-for-Two" List:

Yes, you are reading this correctly. This is the "Honey Do–List" *for two*. This list will help you and your spouse divide tasks and chores during your collective bargaining process.

1. First, start by writing down *all* the weekly "to do items." When all the chores are written, it's easy to see that not one person can handle all the tasks.
2. Next, divide the list. Each of you begin by picking and choosing the items off the list you don't mind handling and then splitting the leftover tasks.
3. Aside from having the goal that not all the household responsibilities are falling upon one person, there is also the goal to have more quality time with each other. Try to split the list to where you both will finish your assigned chores around the same time, so you can have more quality time with each other doing the things you both enjoy most.

The Weekly "Honey Do-for-Two" List:

____
____
____
____
____
____
____
____
____

His List	**Her List**
______________	______________
______________	______________
______________	______________
______________	______________
______________	______________

4. I know it is easier said than done, but once you have mastered dividing your list, try to turn your *weekly* "To Do List" into a *daily* "To Do List." Usually, most of us do not feel like cleaning after a long day at work or taking care of children. So then cleaning falls on our days off or weekends when we should be enjoying our time off and spending quality time with each other. However, completing a few tasks every night can give you and your loved one more quality time together when you have free time, *i.e.*, doing one load of laundry every night instead of laundry all day one day, dusting on Wednesdays, mopping on Thursdays.

The Daily "Honey Do-for-Two" List:

	Mon	Tues	Weds	Thurs	Fri	Sat	Sun
HIS							
HERS							

Chapter Four

The In-Laws: One Big, Happy Family?

Suggested Ingredients: Respect; Acceptance; Understanding; Unconditional Love; Humor; Empathy; Sympathy; and Open-Mindedness.

Tall Tales

One spouse's family is dysfunctional, while the other's family is perfect. One is from the South; the other is from the North. One of you has family members who have appeared on the FBI's Most Wanted List, while the other has family members who own companies on the *Forbes Fortune* 500 List.

One spouse's family get-togethers involve some picnic tables set up in their Uncle Red's backyard with lots of beer, barbecue, and loud-mouthed relatives. Their cousins Ray, Tiny, and Squeaky provide the musical entertainment for family gatherings, and the get-together will last on into the early morning hours until a drunken, heated family discussion results in the intervention of local law enforcement. The other spouse's family get-togethers involve a five-course dinner at an elegant Country Club with fine wine, a live jazz band, and a lovely speech and toast. It will wind down at a respectable hour with coffee and dessert and hugs and kisses good-bye.

With your family, you had no choice but to live with them, spend holiday events with them, and tolerate them. They are your flesh and blood. However, your in-laws are a whole other beast. Just when you finally have accepted that your own family is what it is, you now have this whole group of people you must throw into the mix. There will be a whole new dynamic to your life and family. So, how do you all become one big happy family?

advice

1. Culture shock. In the beginning, it's probably going to be culture shock for you and your loved one to adjust to each other's family. For instance, one may not quite know how to fit into the other's seemingly normal family, while the other will hope to never fit in the other's crazy family. Even when you come from two similar families, it's still a whole new dynamic and group of people with whom you must adjust.

Sometimes, when you just don't come from the same type of family, it's hard to be open-minded. Sometimes, it's hard to relate to the other's family, and it's essentially culture shock. As with any culture shock, the key to accepting your loved one and their family is to try to be open-minded. If you can't have empathy, then have compassion. Realize you cannot change them, nor should you automatically pass judgment on them. You must accept them for whom they are, whether it is accepting that you and your father-in-law disagree about political views, or you disagree with your sister-in-law's lifestyle. No matter what you think about your in-laws or how much you dislike your in-laws or disagree with them, being judgmental and not open to this new dynamic will get you nowhere except creating a family divide and possibly alienation from your in-laws.

While you may welcome alienation from your in-laws, you may also run the risk of being alienated from your spouse. You and your partner accepting each other's family for who they are, good and bad, shows a love and willingness to sacrifice and compromise for the sake of your marriage and an effort to create family harmony. And, like you adapted to the quirks of your own family and initially living with your spouse, over time, you can adapt to your loved one's family's quirks.

It is important to remember that being open-minded and attempting to create family harmony goes both ways. It does not just fall upon the new spouse, but also is the responsibility of the in-laws too.

2. Walking the tightrope. With the above being said, it is not always so easy to just accept one another's family and to keep your mouth shut about things you can't stand about an in-law. It is likely that you are going to have to toe the line of being respectful and sometimes bite your tongue. There is a thin line between giving your two cents about how you feel and alienating your spouse's family.

I'm not saying you should always bite your tongue, but seriously, think about whether whatever you feel is important to say or do is worth it if it causes a divide in the family. The divide being your spouse's family on one side, and you (and *maybe* your loved one) on the other side. So count to ten and think it through before you let words come out of your mouth that you can't take back.

3. Acknowledge your respective family's imperfections: While it is likely not a good idea to disown your family members, or request that your spouse disown certain family members whom you don't mesh well with, the next best thing is for each of you to recognize and acknowledge the personality flaws that certain family members may possess. For instance, if you know your mother can be a control freak, and your spouse gets upset every time your mother attempts to take charge of a situation, simply acknowledging, "I know my mother can be controlling, it gets on my nerves too, and I am trying to find a way to tactfully tell her to mind her business," may make all the difference. It shows that you understand your spouse's frustration with your family member, you too recognize they have that personality flaw, and you are trying to find a tactful way to keep everyone happy without causing friction.

4. "Mother-in-Law" isn't automatically a negative connotation. Ladies, I know. Most of us women can't even get along with our own mothers; therefore, heaven help mothers-in-law. And vice versa, most mothers are critical of their own daughters, so there is no mercy given to the woman who marries their son.

From the daughter-in-law perspective, like female cats, most women are instinctively territorial, and anything that dares to compromise our boundaries and territory, well, *HISSSSSSSSS!* So to most women, the mother-in-law is seen as a threat. This is the woman who possibly previously had the most power and persuasion over your husband. However, once we come in and lay claim to our man and share space together, we want to be the decision makers. But although you've laid claim to this man, you know the mother-in-law will always be in the picture, and at any time, this mother-in-law could over-step her territory. So, like a cat, you cautiously watch the mother-in-law dance around just outside your territory, just waiting for her to over-step the boundaries you have drawn so you can attack.

However, before you immediately shut down the idea of getting along with your mother-in-law, think that one day, it may not just be about you. These rifts can cause a great family divide, not just for daughter-in-law and mother-in-law, but between husband and wife, and grandmother and her future grandchildren—your children. Your husband should not have to be put in the position that he has to choose to be either "your husband" or "his mother's son" unless boundaries have been crossed, you have been disrespected by your mother-in-law, it is creating marital strife, and there is little or no hope that things will ever change. If that is the case, hopefully, your husband will agree with you so you can be a united front when confronting or addressing the issues. Otherwise, such ultimatums can create more marital strife and resentment from your husband than just dealing with your mother-in-law and keeping a safe distance from her. In essence, it may be easier to just be the bigger person and remain respectful towards your in-law, but don't go out of your way to spend any more time with her than you have to.

In the beginning, it may be hard for you and your mother-in-law to adjust to one another, but at least give your mother-in-law a chance. She could have the very best of intentions. If your mother-in-law is a bit pushy or judgmental in the beginning, realize that normally, if you respect her and allow her to see you also have her son in your best interests, as time progresses, your mother-in-law will slowly begin backing away and leave you two to do whatever you want to do and live your life however you want to live it.

Sometimes, we have to remember that in-laws are protective or too judgmental or opinionated, not because of a personal dislike for you, but for fear their child will be hurt or make a poor life decision. Sometimes, all you can do is show you truly love your spouse and have the best of intentions in the hopes that your in-law begins to trust you and your intentions.

5. Surround yourself with positive family support. It is an unfortunate fact of life that some of us will never get along with our in-laws. We will never have that special bond, and it is impossible to have any type of relationship. However, while there may be in-laws whom you will go out of your way to avoid any contact, try to devote spending your time with members of your respective families who do support and respect your marriage.

Although you may believe that family support is not necessary, having support by family and friends can actually increase your odds of having a successful marriage. Purposefully seek out those family members who are cheering for your marital success because when you are enduring hard times, or even just when you need advice on a marital decision, you have family members who can give you advice from their personal experiences. And, you will know they have your best interests in mind because they support your marriage and commitment to one another— especially if it is someone from your spouse's family who likes you and supports your marriage.

Family support for your marriage—like any other situation in your life where you have needed family support and advice, will give you the strength and motivation to work through rough patches and stay committed to your marriage. So don't discount the need for family support.

6. The parental time-sharing plan. Many of you are probably in living situations where you and your spouse live in one state, and your families live in another. For the geographically-separate families, it never fails that the beginning of every telephone conversation with your family or your in-laws will begin with the dreaded question: "When are you coming to visit?" So, like myself and most of my married friends, there is this constant struggle to balance all your vacation time for the year to have enough time to: 1) visit your family; 2) visit your spouse's family; and 3) actually have time to take a vacation. With my husband and me living in one state, and our respective families living in two different states, we are constantly in a tug-of-war custody battle over who are we going to visit. So, similar to divorced parents fighting for time to spend with their children, this results in the creation of the parental-time sharing plan for married, adult children.

However you plan it, I suggest having a couple of celebrated holidays where just you and your spouse spend time together and begin creating your own traditions. For the remainder, alternate between the families. That way, if you spent last summer with your family, and they are upset you won't be home this upcoming Fourth of July, you can explain that you visited last summer, and so this summer, it's your turn to spend time with your spouse's family.

7. Whether by marriage or blood, you are family. We married people all joke about having in-laws, but in reality, it can be a good thing! Growing up, my parents' families had this huge divide. Aside from a funeral, I can't think of a time my mother's family and my father's family voluntarily gathered. However, in my husband's family, whether it is by blood or marriage, *everyone* is family.

I remember the first time we visited my husband's hometown, and his parents hosted a barbecue for us. I was amazed at how so many people showed up just for this barbecue. It was his mother's family and his father's family. Everyone knew one another and got along. That is just how his family is. They enjoy getting together with the rest of the family, whether it is family by blood or family by marriage.

By being with my husband and having the in-laws I have, I have been able to experience what I did not have the chance to experience as a child, an undivided family. I see how family (even the addition of in-laws) can be so beautiful when everyone puts their differences, opinions, or dislikes aside and embraces each other for who they are, good and bad. That is unconditional love. Unconditional love is most felt with family members, and it should be for all family, whether by marriage or by blood.

The Parental Time-Sharing Plan for Married Adult Children:

Here is a way to accurately keep track and divide your time between your respective families. This helps ensure that the time and holidays spent between families is equally shared.

YEAR_______________

Holiday/Special Trip	His Family	Her Family

YEAR_______________

Holiday/Special Trip	His Family	Her Family

Chapter Five

His Friend, the Eternal Bachelor, and Her Friend, the Man-Eater

Suggested Ingredients: Trust; Acceptance; Humor; and Patience.

Tall Tales

Once you're married, your friendships and relationships with your friends will change. You'll make new friends, usually married friends. Sometimes, once you have married, while neither you nor your friends intend for it to happen, you and some of your single friends will drift apart. It is the nature of the beast.

Your status and your life has changed. You are no longer single or dating, and your single, dating friends do not want to be a third wheel. They want to spend time with other single people at bars, restaurants, and clubs. They don't want to hear about your weekend plans to paint the upstairs bedroom or host a dinner for your in-laws. And being married, you probably no longer want to sit at bars full of single people on the prowl.

While those single friends will drift away, there is that one relationship-sabotaging single friend who will stick around, much to the other spouse's horror. For men, it is their friend, the eternal bachelor. And, ladies, you despise him. For women, it's your friend, the man-eater. And, fellows, you are terrified of her.

Ladies, most of you already know what an eternal bachelor is because at some point, you probably dated one and added him to your, "Not-The-One" list. He is your husband's single friend who always questioned your husband about why he was dating you and why he wanted to get engaged. And, once your wedding date was set, his eternal bachelor friend probably conducted a sole intervention, trying to convince your husband that he absolutely should never get married.

Now that you are married, he subtly inserts subliminal messages into his conversations with your husband that single life is the life your husband should be living. This eternal bachelor tries to talk your husband into doing off-the-wall things like spending his paycheck at the strip club, staying out all night, or taking off to Vegas without telling you first.

The eternal bachelor goes through two phases. One phase is his single phase where he has sworn off women and enjoys his time playing video games, watching sports, or hanging out at the bar. During this period, he is rubbing it in your husband's face about how great it is to be single and woman-free. The other phase is his dating phase where he goes through women as quickly as you go through a pint of ice cream. During this phase, he is attempting to prove his point to your husband that he never should have settled down with just *one* woman—you.

No matter the phase, you cringe when your husband tells you he is going to hang out with this guy. Deep down inside, you know your husband loves you, and he will (hopefully) shrug off the ridiculous, relationship-wrecking comments his friend blurts out. But, as women, we are territorial, and we don't want anyone or anything messing up our good thing!

As your husband's wife, you smile and tolerate this nightmare of a friend. However, you look at this jerk, and you cannot understand why, of all people, he has to be your husband's best friend? Why didn't he fall off the face of the earth like your husband's other single friends? You know that if you tell your husband how much you hate his friend and that you don't want your husband to spend time with him, it will make your husband all the more determined to be his friend. Plus, the eternal bachelor will use it as ammunition to reinforce what a ball-and-chain married life really is. So, you wonder and worry whether your husband envies the life of his eternal bachelor friend and misses his single life.

Therefore, subtly, you try to discourage your husband from spending too much time with this troublemaker because you fear he will eventually brainwash your husband into thinking the grass really is greener on the other side. The other side being a single, eternal bachelor.

However, ladies, while you are afraid this eternal bachelor is going to ruin your picture-perfect marriage, there is another force that is equally attempting to sabotage your marriage. That is your friend, the man-eater. I know you are protesting at this very moment, and exclaiming, "But, I don't have a man-eating friend!" Wrong! You just don't see her as *that friend*. You are as blind about your man-eating friend as your husband is about his eternal bachelor friend.

I know you are asking, "what is a man-eater?" You know who a man-eater is, but you just never had a term for her. During your single years, you may even have been the man-eater. The man-eater is single, and no man is *ever* good enough. However, these men are not men whom the man-eater dates. *These are men whom all the man-eater's friends date*. The man-eater is more critical about the men you date than your father. No matter who you are dating, they are *never* good enough, and she thinks there are no good single men left in the world. The man-eater sees all her girlfriends who attempt to date as weak-minded, and she is not afraid to tell them. No matter the man you date, the man-eater comments in a judging tone, "You can do SO MUCH better."

The man-eater insists that the reason she is not in a serious relationship is because she does not put up with any crap. So, you listen to her. And, every now and then, you look at your husband and begin to question, "Is he good enough, or is [man-eater] right, and I have just settled?"

All the while, your husband sees right through your man-eating friend. He recognizes her as a man-eater the first time he meets her and detects her judging eyes scan over him and summarily dismiss him. He is sure that she is subliminally, no, *explicitly* telling you that she can't believe you settled for him. Your husband despises this man-eater as much as you can't stand his bachelor friend. However, like you cannot blatantly tell your husband to stop being friends with the eternal bachelor, he cannot tell you the same thing. So, what do you both do? Secretly, each of you wish, hope, and pray that the eternal bachelor and the man-eater meet someone, and you never hear from them again!

Ironically, this is usually the case. And, when they meet their special someone, you shake your head in disbelief that you ever listened to anything they had to say. You both can't believe you actually thought they knew what they were talking about.

Ladies, in the case of the eternal bachelor, despite insisting that he will never ever settle down, much less get married, one day, out of the blue, he will inform your husband he has met a woman. This will be nothing new (he is probably going through this "dating every woman who will give him her number" phase). However, it will be a good sign if, when he calls the following week, he is still talking to the same woman. Then, to your surprise, it will be the play-offs of some sport, and he won't call to see if your hubby can come out and watch the game. Your husband won't notice it at first. However, then it will come to your husband's attention when he calls his bachelor friend to see if he wants to play golf or something, and the bachelor quickly responds he cannot make it because he has plans with his girlfriend. This response surprises your husband because his buddy always gives him flack for spending too much time with you. However, your husband will shrug it off.

So, this eternal bachelor is missing for several more months, and then one day, he calls. You sigh in frustration believing he must have ended his relationship, and now, he is ready to stir up trouble again. However, to your surprise, he explains that he wants you and your hubby to go out to dinner with him and his girlfriend. So, you all meet for dinner. You are cordial, but it is uncomfortable for you. You despise the eternal bachelor, and you feel sorry for this poor, nice girl whom he probably will dump shortly thereafter.

After dinner, months pass, and you hear nothing from the eternal bachelor. In fact, so much time has passed that your husband actually calls him to see what's up. At this point, your hubby will learn that his bachelor friend has let his girlfriend move into the bachelor pad. His friend has no time for conversation because he and his girlfriend have plans, but he promises to call your husband soon. The eternal bachelor does not call back.

In fact, he falls off the face of the earth and is never available. Why? Because he's in love. He has found "The One." All the relationship-wrecking advice he once thought was so appropriate for your husband now does not apply to him because he has found his special someone. It's now okay to spend all his time with his girlfriend. He's not "whipped" because he turns down offers to join your husband at the bar or a football game so he can spend time with his girlfriend. Now that he's in love, he now realizes that it's okay to be with just one woman.

Then, one day, he will marry this woman. You won't have to worry about being friends with them because they are a married couple, and you are a married couple. The once-eternal bachelor is the kind of guy who marries and is so wrapped up in spending time with his wife, he has no interest in spending time with any of his friends, including your husband. Therefore, you never, *ever* hear from him again.

Now ladies, as you are reading this, I hope you do not have that "I-told-you-so" grin on your face about the eternal bachelor. Your friend, the man-eater, does not fare so well either. One day, the man-eater will call you with earth-shattering news that she is dating this guy, and it is going well. She will want you to meet them for drinks or lunch. Your first impression of him will not be impressive. However, you are not like your man-eating friend. Instead of automatically insisting that he is a loser like she immediately would have told you, you are polite and happy that she is actually dating! However, time passes, and she continues to date this man, and you like him less and less.

You and your other girlfriends begin comparing notes and agree that your man-eating friend could do so much better. You realize this guy is worse than all the guys combined that you and your girlfriends dated, of whom your man-eating friend had so many negative things to point out.

When you all gather for lunch or drinks with your man-eating friend and try to voice your concerns about her boyfriend, she is actually offended and annoyed that you would question her decision to date this man. Ironically, despite all her past judgmental remarks about your relationships, now that it is apparent that you are judging her choice to be with this man, you will hear from her less and less. The friend who was so adamant that real friends don't ditch their friends once they get in a serious relationship will be M.I.A. Your phone calls will immediately forward to voice mail, and she won't reply to your emails. She'll become one of those friends you only know what's going on in her life thanks to her social media updates.

For those of you who have yet to witness this chain-of-events, don't worry. It will likely happen at some point. Realize that once your friends meet someone, and they are in your shoes—in love with "The One," they will see things similarly to how you see it. In the meantime, have faith that if you are with a good man, he will disregard his eternal bachelor friend's advice. But, you have to do the same and not consider your man-eating friend's advice as the gospel.

So try to make peace. And who knows? If you're lucky enough, it's quite possible the so-called eternal bachelor and the man-eater will hit it off since they at least have the desire to wreck your marriage in common. Maybe, they will fall in love with each other, fall off the face of the earth, and neither one of you will hear from them ever again. Then, you and your loved one can exhale a simultaneous sigh of relief.

advice

1. Your B.F.F.s. While you may have a relationship-sabotaging so-called friend, most of us do have a circle of true friends. They may be casual acquaintances, dear friends, or even B.F.F.s. Some friends are best friends forever, and you have to keep that in mind when you take the next step into married life. Just because those friends may still be single or live great distances from you, don't make the mistake of forgetting about them or feeling that you no longer need their friendship and company because you now have the full-time company of your husband. Don't get me wrong, I love to spend time with my hubby just as much as any other married chick, but I believe it is important to still maintain social circles outside your marriage and do things without your husband. It is important to have an identity and life outside being married. And, the same for your husband.

2. Spending time with friends. There is a balance with you and your hubby spending time with friends. It should be enough to give you and your spouse a little space and "break" from one another, but it should not be detrimental to your marriage. You or your husband don't have to be out at the bar with your friends every night of the week, or even every week, but it is healthy to still maintain some sort of life outside your married life. I believe this actually strengthens my marriage. I have the pleasure and enjoyment of spending some time away from my husband with "the girls," but it also makes me miss him a little and look forward to seeing him when I get home. Plus, it gives my husband space to enjoy the things he likes to do when I'm not at home and vice versa.

3. Friendly Advice. While we should at least listen to what our friends have to say about our marriage or relationship, it does not mean it is the truth, their advice must be followed, or their opinions believed. If you ask for the advice, then you should listen with an open-mind, but ultimately, you have to be the decision-maker about whether to use their advice. Whether you are turning a blind eye on your friend's advice or using every piece of advice your friends give you, you *and only you*, have to live with those decisions, consequences, or results that may come from the actions that follow after taking their advice.

Remember, no two couples are in the exact same situation with the same dynamic. Thus, not all advice works the same for all couples.

Also, it is good to surround yourself with friends who are supportive of your commitment to your marriage. I have always found it helpful to talk to friends who have experienced marital ups and downs and can give advice from their own personal experiences about how to weather the storm during tough times in a marriage.

Chapter Six

There is "U" and "I" in "Communication"

Suggested Ingredients: Respect; Honesty; Understanding; Trust; and of course, Communication!

Effective communication can be the biggest booster for a strong and healthy marriage, while poor communication can be a relationship killer. Of course, this goes for everyday conversation. But more importantly, effective communication is a necessity when you are trying to communicate about the not-so-easy topics concerning issues you may have in your marriage, such as things that are bothering you, things that your spouse has done to make you upset, or times when you are unhappy with your relationship. Yes, as men and women, we are human beings. And, more likely than not, you and your loved one probably speak the same language such as English or Spanish or Italian. However, when considering the differences between men and women, it's almost as if we speak different languages. If you are having communication issues with your spouse, you may be experiencing the language barrier between men and women. If that is the case, then you may need a *Rosetta Stone*-style lesson on learning, speaking, and comprehending the language of the opposite sex.

advice

1. Men and women ARE different. It took me a long time to realize it, but an older, wiser girlfriend of mine once told me that, "men do not think the way women do." After being with my husband all this time, I realize how right my friend was. The biggest mistake that we women make is not realizing that men and women are completely different. Yes, we are the same species, but we think, feel, and communicate completely differently.

Remember, as women, we were raised knowing it was okay for us to cry. It was okay to be emotional or moody. We've spent hours, days, probably *years* of our lives discussing our feelings and emotions to our girlfriends, mothers, and anyone else who will listen. Men, on the other hand, are raised a whole other way. Most men were probably scolded as young boys for crying. They don't sit around as teenage boys and young men discussing their feelings and emotions with their dads or friends. They don't have words such as "hurt," "sad," or "disappointed" in their vocabulary. Have you ever watched a group of men watch a sporting event on TV? The only discussion going on involves the game, the score, the bad referee call, what they are going to eat, and whose turn it is to make a beer run. However, a group of women will get together for lunch, but can stay until the restaurant closes by conversing about everything from clothes, work, gossip, and their relationships.

So, ladies, with that being said, as a wife and a female, when you're upset, and you discuss things with your husband about how you're sad, your feelings are hurt, you're disappointed, or you need something, don't immediately get upset over the fact that they seem to lack empathy or even sympathy. Usually, men just don't know how to respond to or speak this foreign language we women speak, which involves expressing feelings and emotions. Although he may lack the ability to respond the way you want, he is probably tore up inside at the sight of seeing you upset, which sometimes comes out by them appearing cold or distant. In reality, it's frustration over not knowing what to do. I'm not saying to permanently let your husband off the hook for his inability to speak or understand your language of feelings and emotions. He can learn if you teach him. But, realize that it may take months or years, *if ever*, for him to actually learn how to comprehend and respond to your emotions or the emotional things you may say.

For the first several years of my marriage, I was so frustrated when my husband was non-responsive to my emotions, or when I would cry. But, I never told him. I would just turn from upset and tearful to being angry and accusatory in ten seconds flat because he would sit there, expressionless, or try to avoid watching me cry. But, silly me *assumed* he should know what to do.

However, one night, my husband and I were out eating dinner with another couple, and my girlfriend and I vocalized to our husbands how frustrating it is that they do nothing when we are upset or crying. Maybe, it took strength in numbers, but my husband and my friend's husband actually admitted that they just didn't know what to do to make it better for us when we are upset like that. Finally, the light bulb went off in my head that my husband wasn't being insensitive; he just never had been taught how to respond to my emotions. And, if our husbands don't know what to do, they have to learn through us telling them what we need. Remember, there is "U" and "I" in "communication."

2. Never Assume. With the above being said about how different men and women really are, you can never, EVER assume your spouse should just automatically know when something is wrong or what it is that is bothering you, or how to remedy a situation without your **express** words. No one is a mind reader when it comes to figuring out what is wrong with their loved one, or why they are upset. And, not all people need the same remedies for the same issue. So, how can you expect your spouse to automatically know the solution unless you verbally and expressly explain what is wrong, and how you think it can be fixed?

I'll give you a great example. I was venting in frustration to one of my friends about how I wished my husband was more affectionate. I explained how I wished that out-of-the-blue my hubby would just grab my hand and hold it or put his arm around me while we were watching a movie. My girlfriend asked me if I'd ever told my husband I wished he would do all the things. Bingo! No, I never explained this to him. So, how could my husband know what I wanted? How could he give me what I never asked for?

Your partner cannot assume things about you either. In the same conversation, my friend, who is not an overly-affectionate person, pointed out that my husband probably just didn't know I wanted him to be more affectionate. She explained how she doesn't need to be hugged or kissed on a regular basis, and most of the time, she's satisfied with just her husband's company. Because she was content and happy with just her husband's company, she assumed that was enough for her husband too. It wasn't until he explained to her that he needed more affection that she realized that he wanted her to be more affectionate. So, while you may be assuming your spouse automatically knows what they need to do to fulfill your needs but just isn't, your spouse may be assuming that because you are not telling them anything that you are content. Hence, the necessity of effective communication. Again, there is "U" and "I" in "communication."

3. Effective Communication. In order to have effective communication with your spouse, you have to learn the style of communication the opposite sex most understands. Generally, men need clear and concise discussions. So, ladies, you cannot have a general, vague conversation about an issue and assume men will read between the lines. Men do not know how to fill in the blanks. Most men see things in black and white; there are no shades of gray. You have to clearly state what it is you need, what it is that is missing, what it is that you think he is doing wrong, or what exactly it is that you both need to work on in your relationship.

As for women, we usually tend to be the exact opposite. We read between the lines. We read more into what is being said. We assume things, and we take things personal. I'll be the first to admit that I'm still bad about doing this at times. So ladies, I personally know it's hard, but try to stop reading between the lines. If you aren't sure about what your partner means, ask for clarification. However, men are pretty simple, and they usually say what they mean.

In order for there to be effective communication, the conditions must be conducive to your partner actually listening to you. It needs to be a time when you can have your spouse's undivided attention, and not when your spouse is about to walk out the door to work, during a ball game or a favorite TV show, or late at night just before bed.

And in the age of modern technology, this communication needs to be face-to-face. Perhaps sending a text or an email pouring out exactly what is on your mind in an effort to explain your uninterrupted point of view may seem like a good idea. **Sometimes**, it may work, but also realize that tone can easily be mistaken in an email or text, and things can be taken out of context. Sometimes, it's hard to look at your spouse in the eye and admit or say certain things. Especially if you're being critical of your spouse or your marriage, or you are discussing touchy subjects or your own feelings. But, this is your partner in life, and you have to reach a point where you can tell this person anything. If you can't be open with this person, who can you be open with?

Most importantly, your communication needs to be non-confrontational. Finger pointing, playing the blame game, and giving ultimatums will lead to your partner shutting down to anything legitimate about your feelings or opinions, and it will make your loved one feel like they need to be on the defensive.

4. Time for a Response. Last, but certainly not least, after you have discussed things that you take issue with, always allow your spouse to respond. And, while your loved one is responding, extend the common courtesy you expected while you were speaking. Listen with undivided attention as to what your loved one has to say, and do not interrupt. And, I repeat, **listen**. Remember, there is "U" and "I" in "communication."

Chapter Seven

For Better or For Worse

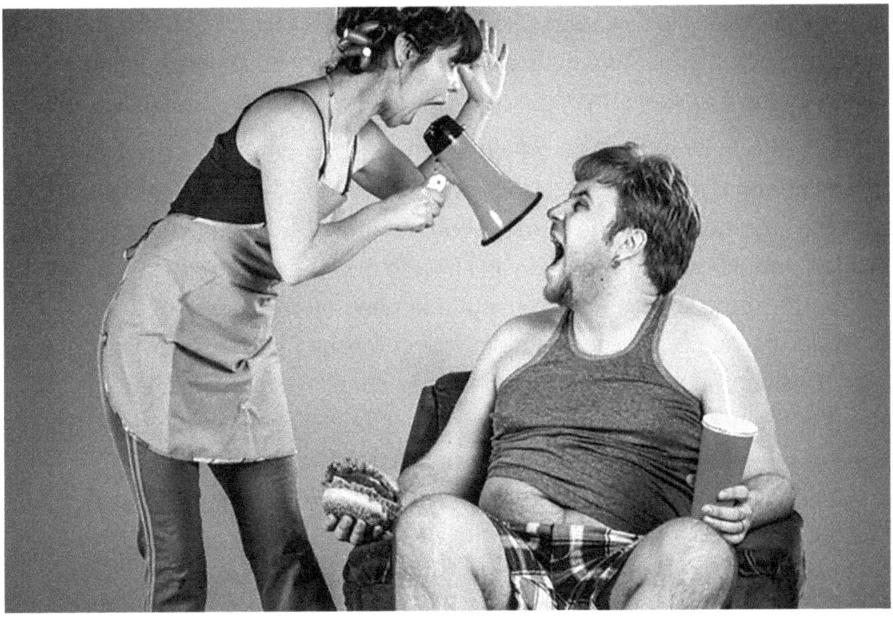

Suggested Ingredients: Commitment; Loyalty; Unconditional Love; Respect; Understanding; Optimism; Communication; and Faith.

As much as you and your spouse love each other, there will be those inevitable phases where you and your significant other do nothing but bicker and argue. You will be sick of each other! The mere sight of your loved one will infuriate you. If you do want to look at each other or talk to each other, it is only to argue. Here are some tidbits to help you get past the worst of it and move on to the better.

advice

1. Pick your battles. In order to not lose your identity and blindly submit to your loved one's views, I think it is good to disagree, *if you truly disagree*. However, it's not healthy to argue over every little thing. Pick your battles. Don't argue just to argue. If you take pleasure in arguing just to argue, when you actually argue about something that really upsets you, your spouse will not take it as seriously as if you rarely argue. When you disagree, or you are upset about something, you should voice your own opinions, try to resolve it, or agree to disagree, and *move on!*

2. Sofa-city nights. When you are going through a phase where your loved one can do no right, this can lead to *sofa-city nights,* baby! Either one spouse, fed up with the arguments and the dismissiveness of the other, will gather their pillow, blanket, and sleep on the couch in an effort to give the other spouse time to cool off. Or, the angry spouse will storm out and sleep on the couch.

Sofa-city nights may go on for days (or rather, nights). However, like children, sooner or later, you will make-up or forget about what you were even angry about (if the husband is angry, he may forget; however, wives forget NOTHING). And, you two will be playing house once again.

When my husband and I were first married, there were a few times where I was so angry, I would tell him to go sleep in the guest room, but he refused. So, I would get angry and go sleep there (And, there was an incident where my husband refused to sleep in the guest room, so I poured beer in the bed so he couldn't sleep there either, but that's a whole other story, and again, I am NOT perfect and do crazy, stupid things on occasion!). Now, I don't do that anymore for two reasons. The first reason is that guest room bed is not comfortable to sleep on, so it defeats the purpose. The next morning, not only would I be mad, but I was tired and sore from having had a sleepless night on an uncomfortable bed.

The second reason is that I realized and respected the method behind my husband's madness and refusal to sleep on the couch. He wanted to prove a point (aside from the fact the guest bed was uncomfortable, and he didn't want to sleep there). He refused to sleep apart to show me that no matter how angry we are at each other, he loved me, and even when it was bad, he still wanted to be lying beside me at night (probably with one eye open).

I adopted the same principle, and even when I'm angry, I don't retreat to the guest room anymore. We may go to bed angry. Tension may be flowing all around us and in between us. Yet, no matter how angry we are, there is nowhere else we'd rather be; we are still committed to one another, for better or for worse.

3. Yes, go to bed angry! Some people say to never go to bed angry, but I respectfully disagree. Go to bed angry! Whatever you are angry about at 2:00 a.m. on a Tuesday night will not get resolved before sunrise, and it will only aggravate the situation. When we were first together, my hubby and I would have some ridiculous arguments late at night, and normally, we were tired, heated, and aggravated, which led to not-so-nice things being said.

Nothing was ever resolved before dawn, and normally, after falling asleep (due to exhaustion from arguing half the night!), things seemed different the next morning. We looked at things differently, had cooled off, apologized for the insults hurled the night before, and worked out our differences. Now, if we are mad about something, we sleep on it, and things look a lot different in the morning after a good night's sleep.

4. A slow simmer. The concept of being noticeably angry at your spouse, but not voicing your concerns, is wasted energy. If you are angry, it seems only logical to air out what you are angry about. Perhaps, when a bunch of little things have accumulated, you are at a point of slow simmering. You are so angry, you cannot even articulate your frustrations. But, that slow simmer will build, causing a boiling point. So, try to not let this anger simmer for days. Just let it out. The days you spend simmering is wasted energy, and it could have been days you could have vented your frustrations and moved on.

5. Damned if you do, damned if you don't: A right to remain silent. (Okay, all you men out there, I'm trying to help you out here so you can have the option of invoking your right to remain silent during an argument or a heated discussion. So, here it goes!) So, ladies, most of the time, when we wives are angry and venting, our husbands don't react or respond. Most men will sit there as if they are in some catatonic state. Ladies, this will add fuel to your fire within. You don't know if your husband: a) is ignoring you; b) is terrified of you; c) realizes that you are right, but too prideful to admit it; d) is simply speechless; or e) all of the above. It could be any of those scenarios, but also realize that men learn early on in a relationship that when it comes to arguing, they are damned if they do, damned if they don't.

If they respond to anything that we say, we'll be angry because they had the nerve to interrupt us or disagree with us. But, if they just sit there like children being scolded and say nothing, we'll still be angry because they won't respond (or rather concede) to our complaints or insults. Nonetheless, men realize if they remain silent, at some point (minutes, hours, days, or weeks later), the argument will be over. Whereas, if they attempt to react or respond to our anger, it will just lead to another argument.

Trust me, I know it's frustrating when you receive no reaction from your husband, but realize deep down inside, men really are damned if they do, damned if they don't. I guess in all honesty, I prefer that my husband says nothing. I just pretend he knows I'm right and has no comeback. And, at least I always get to have the last word!

6. The lesser of two evils. Ladies, your husband has done or said something really stupid and you are enraged. To make matters worse, he will have the audacity to sit there and tell you, "stop yelling." I would be a liar and a hypocrite if I told you I believe it is inappropriate to raise your voice. So, if you prefer to express your anger using something other than your "inside voice," give him a choice, the lesser of two evils: 1) raising your voice; or 2) the silent treatment.

Now, with raising your voice, he may not like the tone you have taken with him, or the words that come out of your mouth, but it's usually a fast and effective way of airing out how you feel about something. You may yell for a few minutes or a few hours, but at some point, you will feel better (or have lost your voice and can no longer speak), and it will be over, either for good, or at least momentarily. So, yelling is a quick and fairly painless process for your husband.

However, the silent treatment, now that can be a slow, painful torture for your husband. The silent treatment can last for days, weeks, maybe even months. It is a miserable process for your husband to endure, and your husband will have to anxiously wait for it to end. With the silent treatment comes watching TV in different rooms, eating in silence or at separate times. There will be extremely awkward moments when he tries to make eye contact with you, and you roll your eyes at him. He will try his best to open the lines of communication by asking dumb questions, but you will respond with short answers in a sarcastic tone (but using your "inside voice" since he insists you not yell). Your whole aura will change, and he will almost suffocate from the tension that has built in the air.

All the while, your husband is sitting, wondering, and anticipating *what is she thinking*? And, what could you be thinking? Perhaps, you are just letting the anger simmer inside, and ultimately, reaching a boiling point where you end up doing the *other* evil—raising your voice and screaming at him. Or perhaps, as you sit silently, you are plotting and planning your revenge in your head.

Of course, you could be thinking anything. You could be thinking of something as innocent as whether you need to stop this silent treatment, and how can you swallow your pride and start talking to him again. Or, you could be plotting his murder. The longer the silent treatment, the more scenarios like this will run through your husband's head, making it extremely uncomfortable for him.

These days of silence will be such a slow, miserable way to end a disagreement, the yelling won't seem so bad after all to your husband!

7. Agree to disagree. Now, you both may be stubborn and will never admit the other spouse is right. However, there comes a point that the battle must end. If you can't have the last word, then, you will just have to call a truce and agree to disagree.

8. Divine Intervention. When all else fails, pray! Never underestimate the power of divine intervention.

Wives' Prayer for Strength during Difficult Times:

Just in case your husband has pushed you over the edge, and you are contemplating murder, this prayer will at least help you make it through the night, and hopefully, "joy will cometh in the morning."

Dear Higher Power:

This has been a difficult time for my husband and me. I know he is my husband, and I have taken vows to be his wife until death do we part. Therefore, I pray that you give me the strength to not kill him tonight, or tomorrow . . . or ever.

He apparently does not value his life as he has gotten on my last nerve and continues to press my buttons. It is not that, at this moment, I value his life more than he does, but I have rationalized the repercussions if I kill him tonight.

At this point, it may even be worth the prison sentence I will have to serve. However, if I go to prison for murdering him, I will forever be labeled as a "murderer." If I ever see the light of day again, no man will ever be interested in me. It is hard enough to find a good man when you're considered "normal," so I can only imagine what my prospects would be now that my husband has driven me half crazy, and after a stint in prison for his murder.

And, although I want to kill him at this very moment, I do love him. So please, give me strength and the patience to overcome these hard times and not kill him tonight.

Amen!

Husbands' Prayer for Strength during Difficult Times:

Dear Higher Power:

This has been a difficult time for my wife and me. I know she is my wife, and I have taken vows to remain committed to her "for better or for worse." However, right now, I can do no right. I have been blamed for everything that has gone wrong in my wife's life (including being blamed for things that occurred before she even met me). No matter what I say or do, I am wrong, and she is right.

At this point, I don't have the strength or stamina to even challenge her as to why it is impossible that everything is my fault. Plus, it will just lead to another argument. I know this too shall pass (and I pray it passes ASAP). So please, direct my wife's anger to someone else like her girlfriends, her mother, or even my own mother, just so things get back to normal.

Amen!

Chapter Eight

For Richer or for Poorer

Suggested Ingredients: Commitment; Loyalty; Acceptance; Patience; Optimism; Communication; Trust; Faith; and Shared Dreams.

I believe it when experts advise that financial difficulties and money problems can be the biggest source of stress and conflict in relationships. Money and debt has always been the number one source of arguments for my husband and me, even before we were married! I can tell you from firsthand experience that money issues will trickle down and affect other aspects of your life, and in turn, create even more stress in your relationship. Hopefully, these financial lessons that I have learned the hard way will prevent you from making some of the mistakes we have made.

short stories and advice

1. Richer does not necessarily mean happier marriage: More money, more problems. Of course, who doesn't want to be rich? No matter how many times we hear it, it is hard to believe that more money does not necessarily make you happier. However, I can tell you, that my husband and I have been through the high times of living financially comfortably, and we've been through the low times of living not so comfortably, and having money does not mean that your marriage and life automatically will be better.

My first few years out of law school, I worked low-paying jobs, which means NO MONEY if you're an attorney with six-figure student loan debt. Luckily, my only major debt was my student loans, but it constantly was a struggle just to make ends meet for everyday expenses, no frills. However, my job was, for the most part, stress-free. Which meant my husband did not feel the trickle-down effects of my work-related stress. Although I did not make a lot of money, we still managed to travel, eat out, participate in activities we wanted to do, and remain pretty much debt-free.

Once I married my hubby, despite the fact I now had his income contributing to the household expenses, I decided it was ridiculous to be an attorney and living paycheck to paycheck. So, I found a better-paying job. Literally within two years of working my newfound job, I doubled my salary! This was huge for someone like me who had been broke since, well, forever!

So, what did I do? I went crazy and spent it! For once in my life, I could walk in a store and buy a designer purse without even thinking about it, and I did! Many designer purses along with designer shoes, suits, clothes, and everything else. Then, when it was time to get another car due to my new commute, I couldn't have just a *regular* car, it had to be a luxury car. All of sudden, our back yard looked rather bare and needed a swimming pool. Oh, and now, hubby needed a luxury car and designer clothes and shoes to match. Plus, there was the organic fertilizer business my husband tried to start that ended in total failure (which will be discussed in detail very shortly).

So, all that extra money was worth it, right? And, more money, nicer things, happier marriage, happy ending, right? Wrong. I have to drive a hellish commute every day to a job where I literally have become a slave to the money. Thanks to the real estate collapse we are still experiencing, we still cannot sell our house in order to move closer to my job. Trying to make more money ended up being a bigger source of stress: my required commute, my stressful job, my now-needed salary, the need to move out of a house (with a pool) with negative equity, the lack of extra quality time due to working more hours, and the lack of free time in light of my work hours and commute.

And, indeed, all of the stress related to what it took to make more money and not handling this new money in a wiser manner had trickled into our marriage, creating a constant source of conflict between my husband and me. In the end, making more money was not worth it. In many aspects, I felt we were worse off. Although there was the stress and fear of not having enough money when I made no money, I really felt we were much happier back then.

I know you've heard it before, and you probably won't believe it unless you experience it, but don't think that making more money is automatically going to give you a happier life and a happier marriage. If you and/or your spouse decide that one or both of you need to make more money, create a stringent set of guidelines as to how you are going to budget, save, and *wisely* use that extra income. Otherwise, you could just be opening up a whole new host of problems, expenses, and debts to handle.

2. Yours, mine, and ours. Once you are married and sharing money and expenses, most couples do not know whether to have a joint account or keep separate counts. My husband and I have found that it is best to have three accounts. His account, her account, and a joint account. Each individual account contains money that can be used or saved at the account owner's discretion. The joint account is used solely for household purchases and bills. That way, it is easy to keep track of personal spending without running the risk of reducing funds for the household expenses and bills. This has proven helpful for us with having individual and joint credit accounts in the same manner.

3. Eliminate as much financial debt as possible. The best thing you can do for your marriage is eliminate as much financial debt as possible. Not only does it take off a load of stress to be debt-free, but it also eases the pressure in other aspects. If you are debt-free, it may be easier for one spouse who is in an unhappy job situation to leave a job, take time off, and seek other opportunities. Or, if you decide to have children, one spouse may be able to just work part-time or stop working during those formative years. Or, if an unexpected emergency arises such as one loses their job suddenly, it may be easier for the other spouse to take over the finances with a tight budget if there is not a lot of debt to pay back.

After going through several cycles of charging up credit cards and paying them off, trust me, being debt-free is priceless. I have learned this the hard way, and

I hope these tidbits will keep you in a much better financial situation because there is nothing more that can truly challenge a marriage than financial stress and debt.

4. The Marital Healthcare Reform Act: As silly as this may seem, if you and your husband have respective healthcare options at your individual jobs, although the monthly premiums may be more expensive, you both should research who has the best plan and consider having one healthcare plan. Don't eliminate the possibility of being on the same plan solely based upon whether your monthly health insurance premium payment will cost more. Instead, judge what coverage you should obtain based on what each of your respective benefits could cost in the event of a major medical crisis, or even ordinary medical care for office visits and check-ups.

When my husband and I got married, we both had healthcare plans through our respective jobs. Ignorantly, we decided that since it would cost so much just to add one person to one of the healthcare plans, we each would just keep our individual healthcare plans since that was the cheaper option. So, for several years, we remained on separate health care plans.

Then, we learned my husband needed a surgery that was not an emergency surgery, but still needed. It was not until that time I realized my husband had chosen the cheapest (and worst) medical plan (like most men would do since they believe they will never get sick, and they will never go to a doctor unless death is imminent). While he had better options that would have covered up to 90% of his surgery, with no deductible, because it was less expensive, he had chosen the cheaper option with a ridiculous deductible that covered only 50% of his surgery, after the ridiculous deductible was met.

I was absolutely mortified at the type of plan he had accepted for several years. As I pointed out to my husband, what if he would've needed an emergency surgery that cost $100,000? But, I was even angrier that I had not taken control and checked into exactly what his health plan entailed. Ironically, although my monthly health insurance premium payment would have been more expensive to add my husband on to my health plan, any surgery, no matter the cost, would cost only $150 out-of-pocket. So from my experience, I suggest that you weigh all your options and certainly don't automatically choose which healthcare plan works out to equaling the cheapest monthly premium.

Luckily for us, my husband was never in a situation where he needed a $100,000 emergency surgery, but had he been, such a situation would have financially destroyed us because of our poor decision to focus only on what was the cheapest monthly premium instead of focusing on the actual benefits.

Don't just research healthcare plans, ensure you have long-term disability and short-term disability insurance in the event of a serious accident or injury. Of course, we all hope to live to 110, and we don't want to think that "til death do us part" will happen for many years, but definitely have life insurance policies.

I have friends whose spouses suffered life-altering injuries just a few short years into marriage, and I have friends whose very young spouses suddenly died. As much as you are probably in the midst of marital bliss, and you don't want to think about it, you must plan and prepare for the possibility of the sickness, the worst, and the unexpected.

5. No Unilateral Decisions: The Spousal Bailout Plan. If you married later in life after you have established yourself and have been financially independent for many years, it will be difficult to suddenly realize you are no longer making sole financial decisions. Husbands will probably not be any happier to see their wives come home with a bag full of shoes that cost $500 each, than a wife would be to see their husband drive home with a new coupe he saw at the auto dealership he drove past on the way home from work.

So, although this should go without saying, do not make any unilateral decisions when it comes to large financial investment decisions that will affect you *and your spouse, i.e.*, buying a new car, taking out a large loan, making risky investments, or taking a lump sum out of your savings. Even if you think this financial decision will affect only you, any major financial decisions should be discussed and made by you and your spouse. If you go down in flames of debt (or money lost) over it, then one cannot blame the other because you both made the decision.

In our case, my husband has always been. . . . hmm. . . . let me be tactful. . . "entrepreneurial in spirit." He reads magazines and books on franchises and self-start-up businesses. His lifelong goal has been to own his own business. I respect that. I too agree that owning your own business is a great thing. Out of the many ideas he has raised over the years, one day, he tells me he is going to start an organic fertilizer business.

Before losing it, I counted to ten. First, I brought up the positive points of organic fertilizer—well everyone loves organic stuff, so that's a good thing. However, I tried to pose some rational questions in the hopes that he would come to his senses such as, what do you know about fertilizer? What do you know about landscaping? Do you have a business plan? How are you going to market this product? What if the organic fertilizer product stinks (literally and metaphorically), and you ruin hundreds of lawns resulting in some lawsuit (that's the attorney in me thinking)?

There were no logical answers to these questions. He didn't even have a business plan. I was against it from the get-go. I never agreed that he should do it, but he was intent on doing it with or without my approval because he was using *his* money. So, he used money from his savings account to start this business, rented a business office, and bought office equipment and products.

And, I am sure you know where this is heading; the business failed. He lost all the money he invested (I guess the one positive note was that we were able to write off part of the loss on our income taxes for that year). Yes, technically, it was his money, but it still did not affect just him. Now, that his savings were almost depleted, the stress was on me because there was no cushion there. I had to take on paying more of the bills, which meant there was less money I was able to save. Therefore, the resentment set in. I was paying for something *he* decided despite my adamant warnings, which led to many heated arguments.

However, after about the 103rd argument over this subject, I just had to get over it. My husband was already beating himself up inside about the money lost. I already said "I told you so" 103 times, so I think he knew pretty clearly that it was a poor decision, and a decision he should not have made unilaterally.

I had to remember that this is a marriage. We all do dumb things and make poor decisions at some point. When my husband met me, I certainly was not in the best financial situation, but he did not hold that against me. So, it was time to move past it and work together to get over that hurdle. Plus, I also had to look back and realize that there were times that my husband helped me financially, and now, it was my turn to take the reins.

Of course, it would have been easy to think that my husband dug this hole himself, so he should get himself out of it. But, that is *not* how a marriage works. This wasn't the time to become divided. It was time to work together and get back on track. Because that is what a marriage is about, staying committed, even during the poorer of "for richer or for poorer" thanks to a dumb decision by your partner or you. And, as time passes, or even upon reflection of your marriage, it is easy to see that it all evens out.

6. It all evens out. There may come a point when one spouse is making significantly more money than the other spouse, or one is the sole provider, while the other does not work. As such, the breadwinner ends up being responsible for paying more of the household expenses. In light of this, some people want to keep score as to how much they have contributed or how much less the other spouse has contributed over the years.

My husband and I fell victim to this finger-pointing early on in our marriage, but as the years have passed, and each of our financial situations have changed, we both have learned to *stop keeping score*! Your marriage is not a business partnership; *it is a marriage*! At one point, you may be the breadwinner. However, it very easily can turn the other way, and the other spouse can become the breadwinner and take on more financial responsibility.

In the beginning, when I was making no money, my husband pitched in a lot and paid a lot of the bills. He paid the down-payment for our house, and he paid off my car for me. Later, especially after the collapse of the organic fertilizer business, he was no longer the breadwinner. I was, and it was time for me to create a "hubby-bailout plan." So, I took over paying bills to help him out. In the end, it all has evened out one way or the other.

Moreover, not everything can be tallied in dollars and cents. If one spouse is staying at home to care for young children, the family is saving thousands of dollars a year that would have been spent on daycare expenses. Also you may be in a lower income bracket for tax purposes because that spouse's lack of income is not increasing your gross income. If one partner takes a lower-paying job because the couple relocated for the other spouse's dream job, then that sacrifice is priceless and cannot be measured in dollars and cents. While you may foot the bills while your spouse goes to school to obtain a higher or better degree, later, when they are making more income, it will probably all even out.

Even if it doesn't even out, a marriage is about give and take, and it is also about sacrifice. If you truly love your spouse, so long as the other is not taking advantage of the situation, it shouldn't matter who contributed what or how much.

7. Material possessions are replaceable. Your marriage is not. The one lesson I've learned is that material possessions are mere objects that are replaceable, and they certainly are not necessary for happiness. However, the sanctity of your marriage is irreplaceable and not something that you can live without to maintain a happy and lasting marriage. Don't let the temptation of so-called prized possessions and material things cause you to compromise your marriage by trying to maintain a "keeping up with the Joneses'" lifestyle.

Upon reflecting on our marriage, my husband and I realized the two primary source of conflict in our marriage has been: 1) money problems; and 2) me feeling that I have no way to leave my job due to the potential risk of loss in income—which I take primary responsibility for because it has been my spending that has created a lot of this mess. So, these are the two things that we need to eliminate from our marital equation. Therefore, together, as a team, and with the support of my husband, I'm taking baby steps to try to embark upon a new career. And, we are taking the necessary steps to learn to live without material things because we both now realize how much happier we were without them. I have recognized that while it is great to have nice things, it is not a prerequisite for our marital happiness. In fact, it created marital strife, and it could have destroyed our marriage. And, looking back to how happy we were when we were starting out together, and we had very little money and things, we now see that having quality, stress-free time together is much more important than any material thing, or even a bank full of money, coupled with the stress resulting from having those things.

My husband and I have survived the business failure. We survived me working for peanuts. We survived my husband working for peanuts. We are still soldiering through the real estate collapse. I am making plans to start a new career path. But, the best thing is that we realized that *together*, we are making it through whatever financial obstacles that arise. Like many couples do, we could've thrown up our hands and parted ways over financial stresses. And in turn, been two single people coping with financial stresses alone.

We have certainly seen better days financially. However, we know we can make it through "the poorer" part of "for richer and for poorer," and we can still come out standing *together*. You can't place a monetary value on that. It is priceless.

Chapter Nine

I Have a Headache

Suggested Ingredients: Commitment; Chemistry; Respect; Understanding; Romance; Honesty; Creativity; and Spunk.

Tall Tales

You worked all day, came home, cooked, cleaned, paid some bills, surfed the Internet a little, and before you know it, it is already 11:00 p.m. You take a shower, lay out your clothes for the next day, and now, it's almost midnight. You need to wake up in six hours to get ready for work. As you enter the bedroom, you see your loved one lying in bed, and they have "that look." You try not to make eye contact in the hopes the will silently retreat. You get in the bed, turn off your lamp, and then they start doing that thing they like to do when they are signaling to you, "let's make love." So, you: a) ignore your loved one and pretend like you are asleep; b) tell them you have a headache; or c) blatantly tell your significant other you aren't in the mood. Sound familiar? I know I've been there.

Maybe it is the routine, or the fact that we just take it for granted that our partner is around, but there is a good chance you may not be as intimate as you were when you first were married. However, just because it's common, does not mean it should be the norm. Here are some pointers so that you and your loved one do not let a brief dry spell escalate to a severe drought.

advice

Five Steps to Re-Igniting that Spark:

1. Commit yourself. To a certain extent, intimacy should come naturally. However, when we have too much else going on, it is easy to move intimacy to the bottom of our priority lists. Like you have to work hard to make everything else in your relationship work, you should work hard to not let the intimacy part of your relationship fall to the wayside. Just like you have to work at other aspects in your relationship, you have to commit yourself to keeping the spark alive and not letting the flames fizzle. Just like you have to make time to clean your house, or make time to go to the grocery store, you have to make time for the things that keep your relationship and bond strong.

2. Night owl/early bird. Sometimes, not being in the mood is not about your spouse, but timing. It may be that your spouse is more in the mood in the morning, but you have more desire at night. So, for instance, if your spouse prefers being intimate at night, and you prefer it in the morning, after constantly being rejected by you in the evening, your loved one may end up frustrated over the rejections when it has nothing to do with them, but more to do with timing. Therefore, by expressly communicating when you are in mood and just aren't in the mood can allow for some adjustments.

I'm not suggesting you and your significant other pull out your day planners and coordinate a schedule, but it is a good idea to let each other know what times work for you and why other times aren't such perfect times.

3. Save the date. If time and tasks are killing your love life, you and your spouse should pick at least one day and one time that you have "alone time." Whether it's a Friday night or a Saturday morning because you are off work and no one is home, or a Wednesday night after your usual night out to dinner, make time. If you stay committed to that time and day, it will become a normal part of your routine without you even thinking about it. While it may seem a bit unnatural at first, it will become a part of your routine, and it will begin to feel natural. But, of course, there should be other times during the week when lovemaking is spontaneous.

4. Time management. As much as we like to believe we have no time for intimacy, most of us have more free time than we think. It all comes down to time management. How much time do you spend aimlessly surfing the Internet or watching TV at night? How much time do you spend texting friends, or gossiping on the telephone?

If we think of our normal day, most of us have more time than we think. We just don't manage our time to prioritize and take care of the important things versus the non-important/trivial things. So, think of the amount of time that you spend on trivial things. If you and your spouse spend less time on these trivial things, you will have more time for each other.

5. Libido lost and found. For some people, not being "in the mood" doesn't have anything to do with not having time. If you have lost your libido, and you want to find it, you may want to see a doctor. Sometimes, low libido may be the result of a medical issue. Pregnancy, childbirth, and monthly hormonal changes can significantly affect a woman's libido. Low testosterone can affect a man's libido. Stress or medications can also affect one's level of intimacy. Sometimes, there are medical explanations for why you feel the way you feel. There are even psychological reasons that a counselor or therapist can diagnose and help treat.

In the times of Viagra and other medical breakthroughs, it is okay to discuss your issues with your medical doctor. Luckily, we don't live in the 1950s, and you won't be the first person (or the last) to voice your concerns to doctors. If you want to find your libido, there probably is an easy way to locate it if you tell a doctor you are looking for it.

Chapter Ten

Ointment for the Seven-Year Itch

Suggested Ingredients: Commitment; Loyalty; Honesty; Open-Mindedness; Communication; and Faith.

"The Seven-Year Itch" is known as the number of years that pass before a married couple may begin to re-evaluate their relationship. People used to believe that seven years was the amount of time it took for most couples to have a declining interest in a monogamous relationship and to potentially consider having an affair or seek a divorce. However, recently, studies have shown that couples actually experience "The Itch" around *three years.*

At some point, some of us will get "The Itch" and begin to re-evaluate our married lives. And, I can admit that for a brief moment in my marriage, I thought I had caught a case of "The Itch." There came a point in my marriage when I began asking myself, "is this really it?" I began envying the lives of my single friends. I felt bored with married life, and I missed the excitement and newness of just dating. I am not ashamed to admit this because I know I love my husband. It was just a little "Itch."

However, there are "Itches" of varying degrees. To most of us, this "Itch" is just like a few hives that goes away within a few hours or few days, and we would never act on our thoughts. However, to others, it is a full-blown case of poison-ivy or chronic Eczema requiring aggressive treatment, of which some believe the cure is having an affair or leaving the marriage. In case you ever feel that you have caught a case of the "Itch," here is a dose of ointment that will hopefully help you get that "Itch" under control.

short stories

All of us in relationships have been there at one point or another; you get in a *funk*. By a *funk*, I mean a boring, repetitive, robotic, zombified routine in your marriage that you just cannot shake. It is the black hole of monotony. I will give you my own personal illustration.

For my husband and me, our weekdays consisted of the following: *Monday*: wake up; commute one hour to work; go to work; commute one hour home; eat dinner; he watches TV; I surf the Internet; we go to bed; and start over again. *Tuesday, Wednesday, and Thursday*: The same as Monday. *Friday day*: The same as the previous four days during the day. *Friday night*: After dinner—take-out pizza—I drink a glass of wine; he has two beers; we begin to watch TV; and by 9:30 p.m., my husband is asleep. *Saturday*: we sleep in late; we go to lunch; we go to the grocery store and the home-improvement store; we grill out on the patio for dinner; I have two glasses of wine; he has three beers; and by 10:30 p.m., he is asleep. *Sunday*: we wake up; I clean the inside of the house; he does the yard work; we eat out for a late lunch; he watches an afternoon game, while I catch up on a movie or take a nap; and we get ready for work the next day. Repeat.

Needless to say, after repeating this weekly routine about 25 or 30 times, this routine became a bit boring. After 75 or 80 times, it was quite frustrating, and after over 100 times, I felt like a robot.

Naturally, I couldn't help but sit and look at my husband snoozing on the couch at 9:30 on a Friday night, and question and exclaim in my head, "Is this *really* our life?" And, while I was stuck out in the middle of nowhere in the suburbs and getting ready for bed, my single friends were down in the city getting ready for a night on the town.

So, here and there, I thought about how I missed my single life (Again, I am not perfect!). I felt guilty because I love my husband, but I hated what a funk our relationship had turned into. A part of me began questioning, "Is there more out there?" Thoughts of separation or leaving my marriage began running through my head. However, as quickly as these thoughts entered my mind, I rationalized about how I loved my husband, and I wanted to know how we could get it back to good. After much soul searching, here was the ointment I found for my "Itch."

advice

1. Re-evaluating your marriage is healthy. I think that re-evaluating your marriage is healthy. By re-evaluating, I don't mean that you should be contemplating whether to have an affair or get a divorce. However, there is always room for improvement in your relationship, and there are ways to stop your marriage from spiraling into a funk. With that being said, it is good to look at your relationship and consider what could make your marriage better, keep you and your spouse happy, and keep the sparks alive. When you feel the funk coming on, take time, re-evaluate, re-group, and have a relationship make-over.

2. The Breakfast at Tiffany's Test. In the late 90s, Deep Blue Something sang a song called, *Breakfast at Tiffany's*. The gist of the song is that a girl wants to break up with her boyfriend because she believes they have nothing in common, and they are growing apart. However, the boyfriend points out that they do have something in common. They both liked the movie *Breakfast at Tiffany's*. So, essentially, the boyfriend is trying to convince his girlfriend that if they at least have liking *Breakfast at Tiffany's* in common, perhaps the relationship isn't as hopeless as she thinks, and that should be motivation to try to work things out.

Well, unfortunately, my husband and I do not have the movie *Breakfast at Tiffany's* in common. I love that movie (and Audrey Hepburn), but my husband fell asleep after the first 20 minutes. However, we have *When Harry Met Sally.* That was one of the chick flicks that I made my hubby sit through when we were dating, and he loves that movie as much as I do. Although we have watched it probably hundreds of times, every time that movie is on television, we will stop what we are doing, and watch the movie together, laughing and blurting out lines.

So, that's where I started. *When Harry Met Sally* is our common ground. From there, there is so much more that we have in common, and it was easy to see that I truly love him and all that we share. Our marriage and relationship was not hopeless.

If you ever feel like you have caught a case of "The Itch," realize that sometimes, we think that our marital issues are a lost cause and something so much more serious than what it is. *Don't confuse monotony with hopelessness.* Think about what you have in common, what you love about your spouse, and what you love about your marriage. Start from there. Use that common ground as motivation and a starting point to stay committed, to work on your marriage, and to break through the monotony.

3. Diagnosing the cause of "The Itch." If you feel that you have caught a case of "The Itch," you have to figure out what is causing it. Many times, the cause is something that can easily be fixed. I again emphasize that you should make sure you aren't mistakenly confusing monotony with hopelessness.

For me, in looking at all that my husband and I have in common, I was able to reflect upon how great and how much fun it was when we were just dating. The more I thought about it, I realized that it was not the single life that I missed. I didn't want to be single again. I loved my husband, and I wanted to be with him. What I really missed was our life before we got into our funk. I missed our life when we lived in the city, and we would go out and have fun together. There was always something different or new to do. I loved my husband, but I was hating the monotony. Once I figured out what was making me so unhappy, it was time to talk to my husband and make some changes.

Try to get to the root cause of your unhappiness or reasons for why you feel unhappy. Once you have correctly identified the causes, you need to discuss it with your spouse in an effort to revive your marriage through "Marital CPR."

4. Marital CPR. When you are in such a funk that you feel your marriage is boring you to death, it is time for some *Marital CPR* to resuscitate your marriage and breathe some life back into your relationship. In order to revive your relationship, you have to express to each other what it is you need: to seek marriage counseling, to go out more, to spend more quality time alone together, whatever it is that you feel is lacking or needed. Your spouse is not a mind reader, so don't be afraid to express what you need.

As for my husband and me, I missed us going out like when we were dating. We never went out anymore. We were stuck outside the city, and I felt like we had no life. So, we began breathing life back into our relationship.

First, we started going out more and enjoying life and activities again. We realized that especially on Friday nights, we were so tired from commuting to and from work during the week, our personal life suffered because we were too tired to travel to any of our favorite restaurants or activities in the city. Basically, we were too tired to do anything. So, we agreed to stay in on Friday nights, have pizza and beer at home, rest, and make plans for Saturdays to go out for happy hour, take day trips to our favorite spots, or spend a romantic weekend away. By spending more quality time together, it made our relationship better. And, it gives us a little excitement every weekend as to what our plans for the weekend will be. And, some weekends, I've found that it isn't so bad just hanging around the house doing nothing so long as we are together.

I don't recommend trying to catch a case of "The Itch," but my little "Itch" led to me voicing my concerns, and in return, my husband and I came up with a game plan that helped breathe life back into our marriage.

Your spouse may or may not be willing to make a change, but you cannot rationalize that you have given working things out a chance until you have explained that you are not happy and why, and attempted a little *Marital CPR* to resuscitate your marriage.

5. Coming full circle. Through all of this, I now realize that wherever my husband is, whether it is the city or the middle of nowhere, that is where I belong. Wherever my husband is, that is home, and where I want to be.

I'm so grateful I never left him at the first symptom of my "Itch" because I thought I wanted or needed a different life. I'm so relieved we worked through things together, and in the end, I was able to see the life I had with my husband was exactly what I needed and wanted. Because, had I left my husband at that first symptom of the "Itch," in the end, I would have realized I already had everything I needed. But, by then, it would have been too late.

We all get an "Itch" for something different sometimes. But the grass isn't always greener on the other side. Sometimes, you see and realize that what you thought you needed to make your life complete—another lover, a change of scenery, or a move to something, someone, or somewhere else that *seems* more exciting, isn't what you really needed after all. Like me, maybe you've taken your spouse, the life you live, or the things you have for granted. So, if you ever catch a case of "The Itch," realize you might just get what you were wishing for, a new lover and a new life, but it may not be everything you thought it would be.

6. The power of love. Do not underestimate the power of love. The fact that my husband listened, and he made an effort to perform *Marital CPR*, showed me that he loved me. That made me feel all the more determined to rid myself of that "Itch" because I love my husband, and I realized his devotion to me to make this marriage work.

Four Steps to Eradicate "The Itch":

1. Re-Evaluation:

Things I love about my marriage:

____

____

____

____

____

The areas where I could improve:

____

____

____

____

____

The areas where we could improve:

____

____

____

____

2. Finding Common Ground: (The Breakfast at Tiffany's Test):

I enjoy doing the following with my spouse:

____

____

____

____

____

The top five things that I love having in common with my spouse are:

____

____

____

____

____

The top five things that I love about my spouse are:

____

____

____

____

____

My best memories of my spouse and me together are:

____

____

____

____

____

3. Diagnosing "The Itch":

Review what you have written in Steps One and Two. Weigh the good and the bad. Identify the cause of the monotony or why you feel unhappy or discontent about your marriage.

____

____

____

What factors or things are causing you to re-evaluate your marriage at this moment? What do you feel is missing in your marriage or needs to be fixed?

____

____

____

In weighing the good and bad, is it worth it to try to work things out? Why, or why not? If so, proceed to the next step, and immediately begin "Marital CPR."

____

____

4. Marital CPR:

Look at what you love about your spouse and your marriage. Think about what you feel could make you and your spouse happier, revitalize and strengthen your relationship, and help you conquer those inevitable patches of monotony. The "Relationship Defibrillator" may help re-charge your marriage. Then begin taking steps to breathe life back into your marriage.

The following could make me happier in this marriage:

____

____

____

____

____

We both could be happier in this marriage by:

____
____
____
____
____

The Relationship Defibrillator

Here are a few ways to give you and your spouse a little spark that may be just enough to begin reviving your marriage:

- Create a date night at least once a month where you and your spouse dress up, go out to eat, and spend an evening doing something you both enjoy, whether it's a comedy show, a concert, a play, or a movie. If you are on a limited budget, spend the evening in, cook dinner together, rent a movie, watch a sporting event, or have a game night.
- Once a month, surprise each other with the most unique gift you can find for $10.
- Surprise each other with cards, texts, or emails.
- Go out of your way to say, "I love you."
- Together, begin creating a scrapbook chronicling you and your spouse's life together. Make goals to capture and collect photos of you and your loved one at unique places or events, or on special occasions and collect memorabilia or "selfies" of special moments. That way, you always have a physical vision and proof of all the special times you have shared together.

List other things that cost little or nothing that you find special that you and your spouse should share that can help revitalize your relationship:

____
____
____
____
____

Chapter Eleven

Tempted by the (Forbidden) Fruit of Another

Suggested Ingredients: Commitment; Loyalty; Respect; Honesty; Communication; Trust; and Faith.

short stories

Early on in our marriage, my husband and I jokingly created a "Freebie List." This was our list of celebrities whom if either one of us ever had the opportunity to have a fling with, we could cheat, and there would be no consequences.

Of course, this list has always been a longstanding joke between us because it is highly improbable, or rather, impossible that either one of us would ever have that opportunity. However, what if the opportunity arose? Not with a celebrity, but what if there was the opportunity with an everyday, ordinary person? At some point, it is likely that an opportunity will present itself. Most of us will shrug it off, or put a stop to any advances right away. Of course, this is easier when we are happy. However, what about when we are unhappy or have a case of "The Itch?" How do we avoid the temptation?

And, as crazy as it may sound to you as you are basking in wedded bliss, it is quite possible that at some point in your marriage, some of you reading this may contemplate having an affair.

Most of us have had that one "old flame." That one former lover whom we felt got away. Whom throughout the years, we wondered, "what if" or "if only we had stayed together." Now, thanks to social media and social networking sites, it is quite easy or likely, that at some point, you will probably encounter that person, or some other person who may appear to be something so much more exciting and attractive than your spouse. So, without you even looking for it or expecting it, temptation may unexpectedly come knocking at your door. And, when we are caught off guard, that is when it's easiest to succumb to temptation.

While, I was experiencing my "Itch," I innocently began communicating with a ghost from my lovers' past on social media. Being that he was now married, and I was now married, I honestly believed we were having innocent conversations and basically "catching up." However, as time passed, the conversations grew more serious, and this past lover began expressing his regret that we ever parted ways. Ultimately, he confessed his desire for us to rekindle our past and pick up where we left off.

This sudden gush of emotions and words completely caught me off guard. And, being completely caught off guard at a time when I was beginning to re-evaluate my marriage, for a few days I was tempted by the idea of starting anew. I began to wonder if maybe this was some sign from the universe telling me that I needed to move on or that there was someone else out there whom I belonged with. Luckily, this literally was a temporary moment of insanity. As quickly as those thoughts entered my mind, I immediately came to my senses and realized this was not the answer to any problems I had with my husband. Running to someone else was not going to make me happier. And, former lover certainly was not "The One." For sure, without a doubt, "The One" in my life is my husband.

I stopped communicating with "Ghost from Lover's Past," and I had to take a deep breath and be honest with my husband about the whole situation. I told him everything from the indecent proposal to the brief moment of temptation I had. This was not the easiest conversation to have, and my husband forgave me. And, of course, I'm so ashamed to think I ever even considered such a thing that it is hard for me to even write this and share this. I could never cheat on my husband, and I never would want to leave him for another man. But, as embarrassing as it is to write, I want you to see just how easy it is sometimes for us to be tempted when you get an "Itch." How easy it is to be tempted when you are experiencing the "poorer," or "the worse," or the unexpected. And, just how tempting it is when you feel that your "happily-ever-after" isn't everything you thought it would be.

In the hopes that you never have to experience the same type of conversation with your spouse, or in the hopes of preventing you from potentially entering the point of no return and actually biting from the forbidden fruit, here are some things to think about if you are ever in a similar situation. Personally, I am so glad I weighed the following below in my mind and heart, came to my senses, and I knew exactly where I belonged—with my husband. Had I bitten into that forbidden fruit, I don't think my marriage would have survived.

advice

Five Factors to Suppress Cravings for the Forbidden Fruit:

1. The grass is rarely greener on the other side: The Forbidden Fruit is probably not "all that" anyway. As I explained, some people who have a severe case of "The Itch" may feel that the only ointment for them is to find someone else. However, beware. Maybe your marriage is not repairable, but don't expect that running off with the first person who sparks your interest to be a quick fix. We all are human. We have eyes, and marriage does not automatically give us blinders when we happen to see attractive people. Even when we are married, there probably will be people whom we are attracted to mentally and physically. And, if you are in a funk in your own relationship, the idea of something new and exciting may cause you to become tempted by the fruit of another, the forbidden fruit.

But realize that usually, in these liaisons, people are likely putting the forbidden fruit on a pedestal (or the forbidden fruit is putting them on a pedestal), and they believe this person is the answer to all their problems, needs, and wants. BEWARE! The grass is rarely greener on the other side. Once the "chase" is over, and the excitement fades, ask yourself, is it really likely that this affair will turn into a serious relationship? If (and that is a huge IF) this affair results in a serious relationship, realize this forbidden fruit will likely have just as many things you will dislike about them as you dislike about your spouse. There will be times that your relationship with the forbidden fruit will also suffer from boredom and monotony. Moreover, while there may be the initial excitement and fireworks over experiencing something new, it's likely it will fizzle as quickly as it happened.

2. The point of no return. Once you taste the forbidden fruit, if you realize you have made a mistake, or this fling was not as great as you thought it would be, and you truly want to be with your spouse, you have reached the point of no return for several reasons. First, if your spouse finds out, and decides to leave you, you have ruined your marriage thanks to a moment of weakness. Second, if your spouse finds out and forgives you, your marriage from that point will never, EVER be the same.

It happens, everyone is human, and some people cheat, and sometimes their loved ones forgive them. It can be forgiven and forgotten by some, but that trust and that bond you once shared has now been broken. It will never be put back together quite like it was before.

Finally, if you cheat, and your spouse doesn't find out, til death do you part, you will have to carry around what you did. Most of us have a conscience, and that is quite a bit to have to hold inside for the rest of your life. Moreover, there will always be the paranoia of what if, just one day, your spouse finds out. So, with that in mind, you have to determine if it's worth it.

3. The Gambler. Before you roll the dice, you need to consider your wagers because in the game of life and marriage, the stakes are high. Are you willing to bet your spouse will never find out? Are you willing to bet the whole farm that this fling will be worth losing it all in the end? Are you willing to gamble that this fling will last a lifetime? Whether this affair lasts a moment in time or for a lifetime, is being with this person going to be worth whatever life-altering events that will follow? Weigh the odds carefully before you place your bet.

4. Through their eyes. In the heat of the moment, people lose sight of the big picture. If you are considering cheating, stop thinking about your needs, wants, and self for a minute, and think about your spouse. Think about what this indiscretion will be like through your loved one's eyes if they find out. Even if you truly believe they will never find out, what are you going to say if they ever do? How will you explain this? Will any explanation be good enough to make them feel any better or forgive you? Will your reasons make them feel any less betrayed? Can you handle the hurt you are going to cause this person to whom you made a lifetime commitment? If anything, think about how you'd feel if the tables were turned.

5. What you see or what you need. Some of us are just visual, and some of us are emotional. Some see cheating as an opportunity, and others like being put on a pedestal. Some cheat because they feel that they are missing something in their relationship. So, if you ever get to a point where you are contemplating cheating, go back and reread the last chapter to determine the appropriate ointment for your "Itch" and try *Marital CPR*.

If you are tempted to cheat because you feel you are not getting your emotional needs fulfilled, then don't try to "have your cake and eat it too." Sometimes, all it takes is just telling your spouse what you need. Remember from my chapter on communication, your spouse is not a mind reader. You have to explicitly tell your partner what you are missing and what you need. So, if you need to hear, "I love you," tell your loved one you need to hear it. If you need for your spouse to be more affectionate, tell them. Your significant other may never be as affectionate as you wish or do everything that you wish they would do, but sometimes just seeing that they are trying is enough to prove to us how much they really love us and how much they want your marriage to work.

Chapter Twelve

Tick Tock, the Biological Time Clock (And in Sickness and in Health)

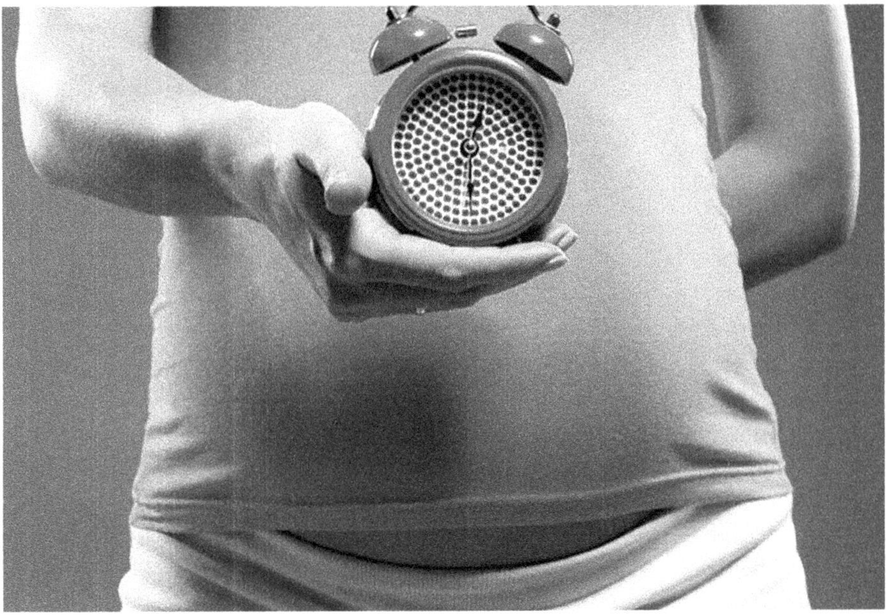

Suggested Ingredients: Communication; Shared Dreams; Acceptance; and Honesty.

Unless you have children right away, be prepared that immediately after your return from your honeymoon, your parents and your in-laws will ask you, "When are you going to have children?" Coworkers and friends are more tactful and won't ask this question until you have *at least* celebrated your first wedding anniversary. *So, when are you going to have a baby?*

short stories

Although I already was in my early 30s when I married my husband, I wanted to wait to have children for as long as possible. Luckily for my hubby and me, it was two years into our marriage before the questions about having children began. We were able to shrug it off that we were not ready. However, by year four, I was entering my mid-30s, and my husband was about to embark upon his 40s. With no baby bump, the pressure was now on. However, our decision to have children was partially by choice and partially due to factors beyond our control.

As for by choice, I always have been indifferent about having children. Being a professional female in our generation, it's a different world. As women in the 21st Century, we are expected to not only be moms, but also contribute to the household income, and still cook, clean, and be a wife. With this new wave of the professional version of Rosie-the-Riveter, we are now expected to be *at least* equal contributors to the household income, while many of us are actually the breadwinners. It is impossible. Something has to give.

So for most of us, we put off having children. We are young, we are busy climbing the corporate ladder, and we are having fun. Therefore, we just keep putting off having children.

And, like most people in our generation, as I started cruising past my mid-thirties (and my husband was into his 40s), there was a nagging sound coming from somewhere in the back of my mind, tick tock . . . tick tock . . . tick tock . . . tick tock . . . Tick Tock . . . Tick Tock . . . .

As that sound became loud and clear, my hubby and I decided it was time to start a family. I looked at my husband, and I thought about how cute it would be to have a mini-him and mini-me walking around. The idea of Little League, birthday parties, soccer games, dance recitals, and having a chance to return to those innocent years by seeing the world through our child's eyes was tempting. We had experienced married life and had enjoyed being just a married couple for several years, and if we were going to do this, it was time.

So, you make love, get pregnant, have a baby, and start the next chapter in your life, right? I mean, when we were in health education in high school, didn't they tell us how easy it is to get pregnant? Well, when you are no longer 15 years old, and 20 years has passed since you were 15, it is not quite so easy, at least for us.

For us, months one, two, and three with no positive pregnancy test was not an alarm. We decided we would just enjoy the trip and let nature do its thing. After months four, five, and six, we were getting a little frustrated. It was time to be proactive.

It was time to start searching the web for "how to get pregnant" (I mean, I thought I understood how to get pregnant, but maybe not). I took the advice of every seemingly reputable blog and web site short of standing on my hands. By month nine, we were getting a little nervous, and by month twelve, we were in panic mode.

Something was wrong. Given our age, it was way past time to see an infertility specialist. Finally, after we both finally came to terms with the fact something was wrong, we gathered the courage and strength to see a fertility specialist. After tests and being poked, prodded, and my husband experiencing the joy of providing samples in cups, we learned my husband suffers from a condition called *varicocele*. Essentially, internal varicose veins have created blockages, affecting his ability to produce sperm. It would be nearly impossible for us to get pregnant on our own all because of something as trivial as a varicose vein. And, although surgery can sometimes fix the problem, most couples have to resort to in-vitro fertilization or other fertility treatments.

As I saw people around me get pregnant so easily, it was hard to accept it may never happen for us. Even for me, the woman who was so indifferent about children. Although I felt indifferent, I also felt I wanted it to be *my decision* to not have children, *not mother nature's decision*.

After the initial shock, anger, and disappointment wore off, I had to start thinking about the vows I took to remain committed, even in sickness. I looked around, and I realized how lucky I was to have found my husband and to be with him. So many of my girlfriends were still out doing the dating grind, and were nowhere near finding "The One." My husband was my best friend, and we had a great life. When we took vows, we promised to be together "for better *or for worse*", and "*in sickness* and in health." So, not being able to have children was a wrench thrown into our life and marriage. But, unfortunately, no one promised we would get everything that we think we deserve.

So, we had to play the hand we were dealt and come up with a Plan B: what our life would potentially be without children. I came to the conclusion that we had to learn to live with the idea that it may just be the two of us. We are trying to fix the situation with infertility treatments, but it has been a financially expensive and emotionally tolling process. And, if we remain childless, we realize we have to be okay with the idea that it might just be the two of us.

It is *not* easy to think this way. I would be lying if I said this isn't heart-breaking or disappointing. I will never forget sitting in my car alone in the parking lot outside of the doctor's office, and bawling my eyes out, knowing that we may never have children. But, this is my marriage to the man I love more than anyone on earth, and I was not about to fold because I didn't get the cards I wanted or hoped to be dealt.

So, now here

we are embarking upon our attempts to correct our situation and try to have children (and that will be a story for another book). However, if and until we get pregnant, we are okay with it being just us, and we have a Plan B of a life *together* if we never are able to have children.

advice

1. Get used to married life before becoming a parent. Like myself, many of my friends married later in life. Many felt that biological time clock ticking loudly and got pregnant right away. However, looking back, many of them wish they would have put the brakes on beginning parenthood so quickly and just enjoyed being a married couple for a while. Instead of being newlyweds traveling, dining out, spending quality time together, and enjoying just being a married couple, right away, it's pregnancy, baby showers, nurseries, bottles, diapers, colic, teething, no sleep, diaper rash, baby proofing, terrible twos, etc. There's a whole new extraneous stressor added to the normal stress of adjusting to marital life. As such, my friends' firm advice to me has been to enjoy married life for as long as possible.

2. Peer pressure. As much as your parents and your loved one's parents want you to have children because they want grandchildren, it's just that they will be only their grandchildren. If you have any children, they will be *your* children. Which means your parents can spend time with your child while everything is good, but can quickly return them to you, the parent, to deal with them when they are not so good. Your parents will spend time with them on average a few hours a week (if even that often), while you will be responsible for them the remaining 165 hours of the week.

Also, you will likely have close friends who will decide to start a family and begin having babies. As a woman, I don't know if it is hormones, pheromones, or what, but the sight of a friend being pregnant or feeling the baby kick inside of your friend's stomach, or holding your friends' babies will set off emergency signals and make you want to have a baby that very moment.

Don't cave to parental pressures, pressure from friends, or even your own pressure. Having a child is a big step that comes with just as many stresses as pleasures, so make sure you *and your spouse* are 100% positive you are willing to take on the tasks and the unexpected issues of being a parent before you try to have children.

3. Brace for the unexpected. Hopefully, you will not find yourself in our predicament, and you will be one of those married couples who get pregnant the first time you try. However, if you end up in our predicament, you are not alone. Once I got tired of being asked when we were going to have children, and I finally opened up to a select few people about our fertility issues, I was surprised to learn we are not alone. We have many friends and coworkers who have experienced or are currently experiencing similar issues. The older you and your friends are, unfortunately, the more common these issues are. However, being open about our situation has given us support and a wealth of resources from those who have been in similar predicaments.

If you are in our predicament, please go in with the mindset that you will be okay if, in the end, it is just the two of you. If you are not okay with that, or if you become obsessed with having a baby as if having a child will be the only way to complete your life, you need to stop, take a breath, and question your devotion to your marriage. Maybe you want a child for all the wrong reasons or feel that having a child will complete something missing in your life or relationship. And perhaps, bringing a child into the picture is not a good idea.

For those of you who do have children, no one has ever told me differently, but brace for the unexpected of parenthood. Everyone agrees it is harder than you ever imagined. However, I am sure once you have your children, it is worth every sacrifice you will ever have to make. So go forth, and happy parenting!

Chapter Thirteen

Everything Else, but the Kitchen Sink

Suggested Ingredient: Humor!

advice

1. Traveling: Ladies, if you and your loved one like to travel, unless you are the type of woman who cares little for fashion, be prepared to hear complaints about how much you pack and how much luggage you bring on trips (which usually husbands are carrying for us). Over the years, I have improved with my packing for travel (I'm down to two large suitcases if I make my husband use a large suitcase so I can fit my extra stuff in his suitcase). And, every time we head to the airport, we cross our fingers, hoping that each of my bags weigh just under the weight limit. So, ladies, I empathize.

Men simply don't understand the concept of needing more than two pairs of shoes when you travel. Men will pack, at the most, three pairs of shoes: 1) one pair of dress shoes; 2) one pair of sneakers; and 3) maybe a pair of flip flops. For us women, it all depends upon what we are planning to wear as to which shoes we will need to wear. Hence, the reason why we need almost at least one entire suitcase just for shoes. Additionally, if your husband is like mine, you are stuck packing all the personal hygiene items because your husband can barely remember to pack his own toothbrush, much less remember to pack things like moisturizer, lotion, sunscreen, shampoo, conditioner, or Q-tips.

So, if your husband complains you have too much luggage on trips, just make the excuse that you are responsible for packing all the personal hygiene items and that takes up too much space in your luggage, causing the need for extra luggage. It seems to work with my husband. He doesn't want to get stuck packing the personal hygiene items, so he gives me some leeway there. When it comes to packing too many shoes, well, that's just a fact of life that men will have to accept, just like when they want to bring their whole set of golf clubs on a trip (yet they never actually play a round of golf on any of your trips).

Finally, if you and your husband have ever been on vacation in close quarters, like in a cruise ship cabin, and you didn't kill each other, you are one step ahead of the game. If you can spend your vacation in those close quarters, living together in an entire residence is a piece of cake!

2. Couples Dates: Once the man-eating friend runs off with her loser lover, and the eternal bachelor friend drops off the face of the earth with his soul mate, there will probably come a point where you and your loved one decide you should find another married couple to be friends with. I can tell you it was probably easier finding your spouse than it is to find a couple whom you ***both*** will mesh with. That "B.F.F.-type couple will have to be two people you both like enough to spend precious time with, and vice versa for the lucky couple. All four of you will have to like doing the same exact things at the same exact time for this friendship to last.

Therefore, the friendship will likely fizzle. But, don't take it personally. It is all that most of us can do to keep our spouses happy, much less keep a whole other couple happy and content. So, sometimes, it's easier to fly solo as a married couple than to couples date.

3. Cooking. Forget the saying "Cook your way to your lover's heart." Show your spouse how good of a cook you are, and do you know what that gets you? The task of cooking for your *entire* marriage. So, remember, "cook your way to your lover's heart, and you'll be cooking till death do you part." I swear, I don't know what my husband ate before he met me. He claims he cooked for himself, but I can count on one hand, really possibly two fingers the number of times he has cooked an entire meal for the both of us during our entire marriage.

Therefore, if you can cook, unless you really want the task of cooking "till death do you part" (or you fear your loved one's cooking will result in an early death for you), I suggest pretending like you don't know how to cook anything other than a frozen dinner in the microwave.

4. Anniversaries and other important dates. In the age of smart phones, email calendars, and other technologically advanced methods for calendaring dates, there is NO EXCUSE to ever forget about an anniversary, birthday, or important date.

And, for your anniversary, regardless how you celebrate, and whether you exchange gifts, try to create a special ritual you do together to celebrate your marriage. My husband and I always watch our wedding video on our anniversary and reflect back on our years together. It doesn't cost anything, and it's something special to help us re-ignite those feelings from our wedding day.

5. The Marital Don't Ask, Don't Tell Policy. Ignorance is bliss when it comes certain information about your spouse or concerning what your spouse thinks. The top questions you think you want a truthful answer to, but you know you really don't want or need an answer to are as follows:

1. Do I look like I'm gaining weight?
2. Am I attractive?
3. Do you like the outfit I'm wearing?
4. What do you think about my mother?
5. Do you think that person is attractive?
6. How old do I look?
7. Do you still think about your ex?
8. How many people did you sleep with before me?

You know that you ***really*** don't want to know the answer. So don't ask!

Additionally, there are questions you ask that you really don't want the answer to because you've already made up your mind like:

1. Where do you want to eat?
2. Do you think I should buy this?

So, for the sake of your marriage, implement your own personal *Marital Don't Ask, Don't Tell Policy*.

6. The Married Couple's Diet: Even when you are a healthy person, who likes to eat healthy meals and exercise regularly, you may catch a case of the "happily married munchies." This is when you are so in love, so happy, and so content with one another, you both begin sharing in the joy of eating. You eat out together, you make cookies, and snack late at night together. You are so busy eating and loving one another, exercise becomes obsolete. Needless to say, you begin gaining weight. Hence, probably the reason there is such a thing called "love handles."

But hey, you're married! You're so happy you don't notice those thunder thighs forming, that beer belly bulging, or muffin top popping out. Usually, at some point, you will come out of your cloud of love, either because the couch is sinking, the bed frame has broken, or neither of you have clothes that fit. Thus, one or both of you will decide you need to lose weight. And, the "married couple's diet" will commence.

Ladies, I want to prepare you so that when your husband drops 25 pounds in two weeks, and you have lost only 5 pounds, you won't take it out on your husband. I don't know why, but all my husband has to do is stop eating French fries at lunch, eat three scoops of ice cream at night instead of four, run a couple miles, and he can drop weight like nothing.

For me, I will eat a piece of fruit for breakfast, lettuce for lunch, and a lean piece of meat for dinner, exercise like I am training for a triathlon, and if I lose one pound, I'm doing well.

So, the key is to realize you can't eat like your husband because on the "married couple's diet," your husband will for sure do better than you without even trying.

7. In sickness: Ladies, I have never met a man who will: 1) admit they are sick; 2) take medication; or 3) go to a doctor. So, ladies, when your husband isn't feeling well, he will complain and whine like a baby. Then, you will ask him if he has taken any medication, to which he will respond he "doesn't like to take medicine," followed by more whining. Instead of going to a doctor, he will tell you he is going to go exercise and "sweat it out." Of course, when the failure to take medication doesn't work, and after attempting to "sweat it out" causes your husband to turn yellow or green, you will be stuck taking him to the doctor and sitting by his bedside while he is hospitalized for a case of pneumonia or some other serious illness.

Therefore, you will have to trick your husband into taking medicine and seeking medical advice. If he is sick and whining, but won't take medication, simply shut him up by saying you don't want to hear about how sick he is unless he has actually taken medication. If he still feels bad after taking the medication, then he can whine all he wants. The second way is a creative way to con your husband into going to the doctor. This is good for at least several illnesses before he catches on. If your husband is sick, and you think he needs to see a doctor, tell him you read somewhere online that an illness similar to his is going around, and if left untreated, it can lead to (pick at least one): 1) baldness; 2) impotence; 3) a decrease in testosterone; 4) genital shrinkage; or 5) erectile dysfunction. The fear of suffering from any of these ailments will outweigh your husband's lack of desire to see a doctor.

8. Shopping: Ladies, never, EVER take your husband shopping with you because this leads to **two** shopping trips. If you are shopping for clothes, shoes, or purses, you will encounter the impatient husband who does not want to wait around while you try on your finds, which means normally shortening your shopping trip. Additionally, anything that costs more than $10 is too expensive, and your hubby will ask you "*Why do you need a purse that costs so much*? *Why do you need so many shoes*?" And, "*Don't you have enough clothes?*"— especially since he now has only 1/10th of the closet.

Therefore, you will have to make a second trip to shop (without him) so you can spend all the money you want and spend all the time you want trying on shoes and clothes and finding matching purses (of which you will purchase, hide in the trunk of your car until he is zoned out watching a ball game or asleep, and then remove the tags and carefully blend the items in with your other clothes, shoes, and purses in your 9/10 of the closet so he does not know what you purchased).

Also, never send your husband to do the grocery shopping. Even with a list, he will forget half of what was on the list or say he couldn't find it. What he does manage to purchase from your list, it will be the wrong brand or wrong type of food like Muenster cheese instead of Colby Jack Cheese, and white bread instead of whole wheat. Moreover, he will insist that it was appropriate to buy only the generic brand of whatever is on your list, which means he may bring home some scary brand of detergent named something like *Sudz* that will fade all your clothes. Thus, asking your husband to go grocery shopping only prolongs the inevitable— you having to return to the grocery store to pick up the items you needed.

9. The Pride Syndrome: Ladies, every man I have ever encountered suffers from "The Pride Syndrome." I am not talking about having too much pride to cry. Or, even too much pride over his perfectly manicured lawn. It is a fact of life, so don't try to change him, but every man has too much pride to:

1. Ask for directions;
2. Ask for help at a home improvement store;
3. Admit that they need assistance assembling something;
4. Admit that they don't know what the car mechanic is talking about when your car is in need of repair;
5. And, heaven forbid, admit that you are right about something, and he was wrong.

All you can do is realize that to them, it is too emasculating to admit they need help in these categories, especially if you are present. All you can hope for is that GPS will eventually get you to your destination; somehow you will happen upon the item you are looking for at the home improvement store; whatever your husband assembled, will not come crumbling down (but if it does crumble down, it deservingly should crumble down on your husband's head); and that your car will be adequately repaired without the need to take out a second mortgage.

Well, I think that covers about everything, but the kitchen sink, that I have experienced along the way to happily-ever-after. Now, let's talk about "happily-ever-after. . . ."

Chapter Fourteen

Happily-Ever-After?

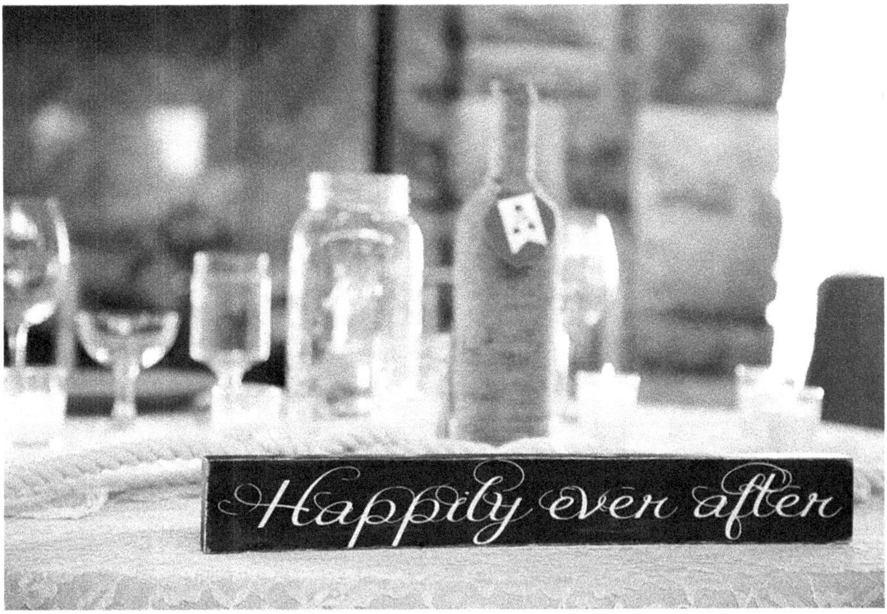

Suggested Ingredient: Eternal Optimism.

As married couples, it seems like we are all striving to live happily-ever-after like in the movies and fairy tales. Even in the movies, we never actually see what "happily-ever-after" is. So, *what* is "happily-ever-after?" Sometimes, I think back to mine and my husband's favorite love story, *When Harry Met Sally*. I wonder if Harry and Sally really existed, would they live happily-ever-after? Where would they be now? Would they still be happy and in love, or would they be just another statistic where they fell madly in love, but later, fell out of love and divorced?

Perhaps after five, ten, or fifteen years, Sally grew tired of Harry's obsessiveness with pessimism and morbidity? Or, Harry lost patience with Sally's perfectionism? Even in the movies and fairy tales, is there happily-ever-after?

So, for us everyday people who live in the real world, does happily-ever-after really exist? Or, perhaps the better question is, *what is happily-ever-after*?

Now that over seven years has passed since my husband and I were married, and we have traveled down this path towards this so-called "happily-ever-after," with ups and downs and everything in between, my idea of "happily-ever-after" has changed. Like most people, our marriage is far from perfect, and it certainly hasn't been smooth sailing like I hoped and dreamed it would be. However, even when there has been the worst, the poor, and the moments of unsureness, in the end, my husband and I still come full circle and know we are exactly where we belong—together. Even with the not-so-happy times, we have seen many more days of happy and ups and the better. Plenty of days with laughter and joy. And always, a love for one another I could not have for anyone else.

I'm still learning something new every day. I'll still make mistakes, and I will never be perfect. And, the same goes for my husband. However, even with no Hollywood-style happy ending, most of us see that we can still be happy, still have great times, still be madly in love, and still be committed to our marriages.

I believe that happily-ever-after does exist, and I believe I already have happily-ever-after. There are days I look at my husband and go into a fit of rage over something stupid he has done. However, there are days I look at him, and I can't believe how amazing he is, and I am so thankful he is a part of my life. That is my happily-ever-after. There are moments where we get hysterical over the silliest little thing, both laughing uncontrollably. That is my happily-ever-after.

There are moments when something good or bad happens, and he is the first person I want to talk to, and I find comfort in just talking to him. That is my happily-ever-after. Just six months after we were married, my father suddenly died from a heart attack. I will never forget leaving the funeral home so grief-stricken, I think I would've collapsed had I not had my husband there to hold me up and console me. Literally having someone there who "has my back" in my worst moments of despair is my happily-ever-after.

There are our Friday nights when I look forward to my husband coming home with pizza and beer so we can spend the evening watching television and planning our weekend. That's my happily-ever-after. There's every single morning when he leaves for work and does not walk out the door without coming to my bedside and kissing me (despite my morning breath) and telling me that he loves me. That is my happily-ever-after.

There is nothing I love more than when I have dozed off to sleep while we watch TV in bed, and instead of nudging me and waking me up to turn off my light, my husband will get out of bed, walk all the way around the bed to my night stand and turn off my night lamp for me. He gets in the bed, puts his arm around me, and we go to sleep (with our two cats and dog asleep at the foot of the bed). Lying next to the man I love more than anyone on this earth and knowing this is exactly where I belong, that is my happily-ever-after.

To me, "happily-ever-after" is not this utopia of love, happiness, and perfection that we all seem to strive for. My happily-ever-after is finding someone who loves me just the way I am, imperfect and all, and who loves me throughout the times, good times and bad. My happily-ever-after is being 100% sure that being with my husband is exactly where I belong, and there is nowhere else I'd rather be.

Happily-ever-after is knowing there is someone whom we loved, and no matter what happened, that person loved us enough to join hands with us and travel through this journey of life together. In my life, without a doubt, that person is my husband, and without a doubt, I found my happily-ever-after.

May you and your loved one find happily-ever-after . . . .

advice

You have heard enough from me! Now, it is time to hear advice from other married couples who are wiser, and who have been married for much longer than I have. I asked my closest friends and family, who have been married for many years, to share their advice. I had no idea what would be written, and I assumed everyone would give the same generic advice. However, what I found so intriguing is that each couple had different and unique pieces of advice that works for them and different ideas about what "happily-ever-after" meant to them.

So, here is their advice for you, their lessons learned, and their ideas of "happily-ever-after." I hope that throughout my book, you have found bits and pieces with which you can relate and can help you in your relationship and marriage. And, I hope you also find inspiration through my friends' and family's stories.

Marie and Joe

Married 52 years

We have been married for 52 years. Although we were not always compatible some of those years, we made it through. We think to make a marriage last, you need: respect for one other; to become each other's friend; have good communication; and have a good sense of humor.

Our advice: "Don't sweat the small stuff!"

Example: We used to quarrel over which way to place the toilet paper on the holder, over or under.

She says: "It will roll better underneath."

He says: "It makes no difference."

Compromise. It is a partnership.

Happily-ever-after for us as an elderly couple is having good health and watching our family and the next generation grow.

Marie and Joe

G and P

Married 42 years

I look around and cannot believe have been married for forty-two years (I was only 5 when I got married!). I'm also amazed that I had the wisdom at sixteen years old to pick the guy I did, that he went along with it, and that everything has lasted, strengthened, and only gotten better.

Growing up, I lived on Main Street in a typical small New England town, so I saw a lot of sights driving by my long front porch. In the spring of my junior year of high school, while sitting on that same porch, I noticed a really cool guy driving a really cool car (a brand new 1969 Z-28 Camaro) and eating an orange Popsicle. My first thought was that he couldn't be all that bad if he would be driving that car and eating a sticky, melting orange Popsicle at the same time!

Fast forward a few months to August just before I was about to enter my senior year of high school. We both ended up at the same restaurant and got to talking and decided to go to a movie. After a few dates, we decided to take a ride on the newly built interstate highway that had yet to open for regular traffic. Bear in mind I had the family car that I left at the same restaurant where we first talked, and he was driving the Z-28.

Foolishly, I did not take the family car home before we went on our little drive on the new highway. To make a long story short, I was grounded for getting home late (sometime after midnight) and causing my mother to worry about my wellbeing. Well the grounding didn't work, and I snuck out to meet my boyfriend and magically, love bloomed between us. I knew from that point on he was the one I would marry.

We both always had a love for cars and anything that would go fast, so that was, in large part, why our relationship blossomed. Based on my personal experience with marriage, couples need to have common interests to keep the spark of marriage alive and want to do things together. I know there is no one I would rather spend time with than my husband, and I know he feels the same way about me.

We also share the love of dogs and welcomed our first of five Great Danes into our lives after we had been married a couple of years. This new chapter took on a whole new meaning as we were proud new "parents" and soon-to-be homeowners. We had grand ideas on how we would raise our little Daisey and not spoil her. For instance, she would not get in the bed with us! Ha, did not happen. I came home one night and found her fast asleep with her head on my pillow. She would not eat people food; you know that one never works. And, the big one, in her case at least, she would not chew wood. Sure, when you're struggling to build a dog house tall enough that even a Great Dane would not be able to jump over and she won't let you get the job done, you throw a little piece of 2x4 wood for her to play with. Bad, bad, very bad idea. From that point on, for the rest of her life, anything wood had her bite mark on it.

Many times in a marriage, the in sickness and in health part of the vows, especially the sickness part, never become an issue. Well, sadly that was not the case for us. We were put to the test six years into our marriage when my husband had a serious accident that left him paralyzed and needing a wheelchair. To say our lives were turned completely upside down would be an understatement. We both had good jobs, each had our own car, and our first home. Everything right was supposed to be happening for us.

Once the accident happened, we were on our own with little support from our families because they did not live close by and were older with their own medical issues. Facing something like this together made us even closer and gave us strength to face challenges I never could have imagined. When you are truly in love with someone and something like this happens, you would hope it makes the marriage stronger. Not always the case. It can put too much strain and may end the marriage because one or both simply cannot cope with the tragedy. I am so grateful this did not happen to us.

Trust is a larger part of being a couple. My idea of trust is someone who I don't have to think twice about handling the money and helping me make choices and decisions that would impact our future together. There is no one on earth I trust the way I trust my husband. I have complete faith in his judgment and the guidance he gives me when it is time to make a life-altering change. Whether that would be a significant move from one part of the country to another that we accomplished very successfully over thirty years ago, deciding to build a new home (not once, but twice!), or me making a job change, we always discuss everything, making a list of pros and cons to help us decide and make decisions together.

One of my biggest decisions I have had to make came last year when I decided it was time for me to retire from a very stressful job and place the priorities in my life in the order they should be in. My husband was right there, encouraging me every step of the way and reassuring me that yes, we had done the right thing for all these years, that yes, we would be all right, and that yes, I could and should do this, and that it would be the best thing for both of us.

I had some doubt that maybe it was not the smartest thing I had ever done from a financial standpoint, but he kept assuring me that it was the right time and that we would have a comfortable life and that everything would be all right and turn out the way it should. In the time I have been retired, I have been pleasantly surprised at how right he was about everything. It wasn't that I didn't trust his wisdom and advice, I was just unsure of how things would work with us spending so much time together after all the years of spending so much time apart while I was working.

With no major health issues facing us and enjoying life together, our future is bright and full of promise. All because of a very long, deep love for each other and good, sound judgment and sense on how to live our lives.

I can honestly say there is nothing I would have done differently in my life; how often can people say they don't have some kind of regret? Things have happened to us because they did; we could have made a choice or not. I am grateful that we were able to make the most of things that have come our way and move on to the next chapter.

P.

Jennifer Anderson and Raymond Haight

Married 15 years

Everyone has their own idea of what a good marriage is, and what makes it last. You'll get a thousand different pieces of advice, and they are all probably good, but you will have to sift through and find what works for you and your spouse, and maybe make your own advice along the way. I can only tell you what works for us and pass it on. Ray and I have been married for 15 years, so something must be working for us.

1. If you both work, have separate bank accounts. *Money is the number one argument amongst couples. One spouse is upset about how the other spends. money, and what they spend it on. We have figured out a household budget We know how much we need to put in each month to keep the household running, and anything is left over, we keep it and spend it as we please. We have not had one fight about money.*

2. Have a sense of humor. *Lots of things come up during a marriage, and if you can't laugh through them, marriage will be tough. We both have lost a parent, and it has been healthy for me and him knowing we can always find a way to inject humor into a situation. If you as a couple can't do this, your marriage will end up being in a dark place, rather than a place for comfort and stability.*

3. Marry your best friend and WANT to spend time with them. *Ray is truly my best friend, and I his. We talk about everything and look forward to spending time together. If you are dating someone and thinking about marriage, and you don't call the person you're marrying your best friend, think twice. I truly enjoy spending time with Ray. Don't get me wrong, I like a night out with friends too, but they are rare because I would just rather spend time with him, even if it is just dinner at home and TV on the couch.*

4. Set physical boundaries for each other. *Let me explain. Being married does not mean when I come home from work, you're glued to my hip wondering what we are going to do together. Give each other space and take a breather from everyone, including you. This does not mean having drinks with the girls or boys every day after work. It means be stable enough within yourself to realize I am not in this marriage to entertain you, so let me decompress, alone. Ray is super about this. He can read me very well, and if I am having a bad day, he lets me sort it out first on my own, and then lets me vent, but he gives me time to take a breather. This is the best thing he does for me, and I appreciate it.*

5. Separate bathrooms. *If you can't do this, then at least two sink areas. You will thank me later. It is true bliss.*

Jennifer Anderson

Marianne and Paul

Married 13 years

When I was asked to write something about "marital advice," I said to myself, what did I have to offer? I have been married twice. My first marriage lasted 19 years, gave me two wonderful sons, yet was a very abusive situation. I'm remarried and approaching my 14th anniversary. My husband now is the exact opposite of my first. Thank God. But I have learned so much from both marriages.

From my first marriage, I learned how to detect abuse and realized I was the stronger person in that marriage. I ask myself continuously, why didn't I run? I still can't answer that question, but I certainly can help others detect psychological abuse and help them realize how strong they are and how they can go on without the abuser. And most of all–there is life after that, and I deserved much better. I was one of those who deserved better, and I found life.

My current husband, Paul, his love fed me life, trust, and security. And I grew into the woman I should have been 20 years before. He had tremendous patience with me as I learned how to love and, most importantly, be loved. I had to learn quickly that in order to keep Paul, I could not judge him on the only experience I had, that of abuse. But he hung in there and communication saved our relationship. I had to learn to open up and not fear retribution for something that was nonexistent. Paul learned early in our relationship that he had to pull things out of me and not think I was doing something strange or unfounded but that I was protecting myself, and I slowly learned that my self-protection was no longer necessary. Communication and patience got us through.

I don't look back. I've learned to enjoy life now and share what I have learned along the way. What did I learn? The most important thing in my marriage is communication. Communication in all forms, most importantly, honesty and laughter. Paul loves to make me laugh and that laughter has helped to heal my soul. One of his favorite things is to come up on me and scare me, which I must confess, isn't too difficult. He can scare me by just walking into a room. Seriously, if I turn around and he's there unexpectedly, I jump. And he laughs, and that laughter is contagious. Even though I feign being upset, it is seriously extremely hilarious. And this continues to this date, 14 years into our relationship and I can still be jolted out of my skin so easily. It's that type of conversation, yes conversation, that keeps our marriage fresh, happy, and loving.

Communication in all forms, a smile, a wink, a quick hug that is the glue to our Happily-Ever-After.

Marianne

Janis Wilson Hughes and Rob Hughes

Married 11 years

Janis Wilson Hughes & Rob Hughes were married on the beach in Punta Cana, Dominican Republic in April 2003.

You know that saying that goes, "just when you least expect it, just what you least expect?" That's how it was when I met my husband. I had spent my early 20s constantly on the lookout for "The One," and along the way, I had wandered into deep unhappiness with most other parts of my life. By my mid-20s, I was miserable in my job and desperately unhappy, living in the area I had relocated to for that thankless job. I had only two priorities at the time he came along. Priority One: Move somewhere warm and sunny (with or without a job) and never return to the land of my discontent. Priority Two: Get a better job.

One day at work, I was told to meet with a guy to track down the source of some reporting problems. My future husband was introduced to me with no fanfare, no fireworks, no twitching of the romance-sensing antennae. We got along fine and even bonded over some mutual work frustrations. We began to hang out and eventually started dating. Ironically, my husband is probably the only man I ever dated with expectations that it would only be short-term, and we would not have a future. He was in direct conflict with my priorities. For all intents and purposes, he was a local boy, and all I wanted was to get out of Dodge. Why would I even consider tying myself down to anyone local?

But because I wasn't afraid of pushing him away, I was open and honest about all my most fundamental beliefs, which I might not have brought up so early on or communicated as decisively otherwise. Having open discussions on things like religion, children, and political views early in our process of getting to know each other meant those things weren't lurking ahead in the road, waiting to trip us up. In fact, the better we knew each other, the more we liked each other. My husband is the only guy I dated who I liked more and more over time. Based on this early foundation, we both believe open discussion about any relationship issue that's weighing on our minds is important. I know that sounds obvious, but truly it's something you have to work at.

There's always a temptation for avoiding conflict, and it may seem like there's never a good time to bring up a topic that is emotional or uncomfortable to talk about. If it's weighing on your mind, that's probably because you worry your spouse doesn't have the same view you do. Don't fool yourself that you can brush it under the rug. It will come out at some point. It's best if it comes out when you are emotionally in control and not reactionary, defensive, or attacking.

When we met, we had very different political views and priorities with money. We were open about it, though. We didn't pretend to agree. By talking through the nuances of our viewpoints, we found there was a lot of common ground and neither of us had to change to get along. Thankfully, though, he was open to moving, because my Priority One was non-negotiable!

Control is a very dangerous mine field in relationships. No one likes to be controlled. And if you build your happiness on being able to control your mate, you will have serious issues. It's hard when you see your mate doing self-destructive things like eating poorly. You want to tell them to stop. When that doesn't work you want to make them stop. You start getting upset. Then your mate gets upset from the nagging. It doesn't go anywhere except making you both angry.

It's a hard lesson to truly accept, but here at the 11-year mark in our marriage, I have accepted that I can't control my husband, and when I try to, it just makes us both unhappy. Instead, I try to positively influence him by encouraging all the good stuff. But I let go of trying to control him. The simplest truth is that I am the only thing I can control.

An extension of the desire for control is an attitude of, "I can't enjoy doing something unless you think it's fun too." That's unfair pressure to put on your mate. It's great to have shared hobbies, but don't feel like you can't have your own interests as well. Yes, you're married, but you're still separate people. If there's something in your life you need to do to feel self-actualized like learning to speak Italian since your grandparents were Italian, then learn to speak it on your own if your mate isn't interested in learning it too. Don't force them on the journey with you, and don't feel like you can't do it because they won't do it with you. Do your thing! It's good to have some independence. By shining your light and growing as a person, you'll probably make your mate proud, happy in seeing your happiness, and possibly even inspired by your accomplishments.

And speaking of happiness, a little bit of thanks and appreciation goes a really long way. Didn't your momma teach you any manners? For goodness sake, show your spouse the same courtesy you would to a stranger who helped you pick up something you dropped. Don't forget to say "thank you." Just because there are things that have to get done around the house doesn't mean that we shouldn't express thanks to each other for doing them.

Even though I enjoy cooking, when my husband gives me a heartfelt thank you for making him dinner, that makes me feel great! By the same token, I thank him for restocking the toilet paper in the bathroom. Thanking your mate for the everyday things they do is such a simple thing that makes a world of difference.

As I approach 12 years of marriage, I am happier than I was before I was married. And I believe my husband would say the same thing. For me "happier ever after" might be the goal instead of "happily ever after." Of course, we still have disagreements, and we have a couple of ongoing issues we have worked on for a long time. But even so, we long to have more time to spend together. We have mutual hobbies and enjoy making each other laugh. We can be our true selves with each other, and even if he can't relate to my experience or feelings, he still accepts them and vice versa. On a day-to-day basis, I'm certainly happier than I was before I was married. And that to me is success.

Janis

Tomeka Jackson-Chance and Anson Chance

Married 11 years

My name is Tomeka Jackson-Chance, and I have been married to my husband, Anson, for 11 years. My husband is 46, soon-to-be 47, and I am 39. The first few years of marriage were really challenging because my husband was always used to his mother doing things for him. His contribution to a different home life was difficult and we so desperately needed to change that and make him a little more responsible. This was important to me because I was working, attending school to finish my degree, and had a child we needed to care for and give our undivided attention to. Adjusting to this new life often created tension between us, but he learned and we made it work.

There are times when you want to throw in the towel, but when making that decision, make sure it is the best decision for everyone. When couples become one through marriage, you say those vows with the intent of having a happy life and being together forever or A'till death do us part. So, how do you make a happy marriage? Communication is one key to the whole thing. You have to make time to talk to each other even when something you are about to say, the other may not like. For example, I needed to discuss with my husband the decision to purchase a car. A Mercedes Benz to be exact. The conversation got heated and afterward, my husband and I did not talk for days. Finally, I went to him and asked, "Why do you not want me to buy this car?" He simply explained that he didn't want us to live beyond our means and making such a big purchase would set us back on the goals we are trying to achieve financially. He made perfect sense and I re-thought my move for the car. The point I am making is you can't make decisions like this on your own without consulting your spouse because your decision can sometimes benefit the family or set the family up for failure.

Anson and I are working people making our way day-to-day. Our household income is middle-class, and sometimes we get to splurge a little here and there. How do we get through the times when there is not enough money? We cut back on things that are unnecessary. Instead of spending money on a night out to dinner, we find things that we can make at home and use that money we would have spent on a night out to put it toward paying off some other debts that we have. I lost my job after almost 12 years of employment, and I was unemployed for over two years. It really taught us a lesson. We had to work with what we had for the moment, but it also taught us to live within our means. My husband never really complained about me being laid off for so long. You learn to work through your money issues and better manage your finances for the best interest of the family as a whole.

Making the marriage last, again, is through communication but the most important way is through T-R-U-S-T. Trust is the glue that holds the two involved together. Before my marriage to Anson, I had a few trust issues because I had been hurt so many times before. Getting involved with men who only wanted me for what I could help them do rather than helping us both "do." My husband gives his all when it comes to me and I return the favor to him. I don't watch his every move because we can't be together at all times. When we are away from each other, we check in to make sure the other is okay. I go on trips without being in fear that he is being unfaithful and vice versa. Also those times when I am away from him for days, it brings us closer and helps me to understand why we love each other so much, which is the reason we stay together.

My advice to anyone is you can't change everything about a person because as my father always said, "You can't raise a person twice." Once someone gets to the adult stage, what they have learned to that point will always exist. You can only hope that you can break old habits. There are things your spouse will do that will make you mad, and you will have many disagreements, BUT that is not the reason to call it quits. Nowadays, people give up so easily because they think that nothing they are putting into the relationship works. What you can do is don't just look at the things you think your spouse should be changing, but also turn to yourself and ask, "Is there something about me I need to change?" Once you answer this question, maybe you can make your relationship last despite the few disagreements you may have here and there.

My happily-ever-after is achieving the goal of staying together. My love has definitely matured for my husband over the years. I'm not saying that I never loved him or that we married for other reasons. We have learned to watch what we say and do to each other, being careful not to hurt feelings and develop hatred that would not lead to a happily-ever-after. So often when it's time to do the laundry, I'm all done for the day and I'm putting it away. If I look and find some dirty socks that did not make it in the laundry, I shouldn't get mad. I should just let him know that he'll be the one doing any extra loads because my chore is done. He may think it's unfair, but he'll learn to make sure all pieces of clothing are there when it's laundry time. He's everything to me, and I say to people often that I wouldn't trade him in for the world!!

Tomeka Jackson-Chance

www.ingramcontent.com/pod-product-compliance
Lightning Source LLC
Chambersburg PA
CBHW070833100426
42813CB00003B/606
9780692436721